Southern Living

COUNTRY ★ MUSIC'S GREATEST EATS

★★★★★★★★★★★★★

PRESENTED BY

CMT

Oxmoor House

A NOTE FROM THE AUTHOR

In the conversations I had with the country music stars and personalities that are spotlighted in this book, the minute I asked them about their favorite dishes, I heard the audible "Mmmm" that love and happy memories evoke. After a while I began to expect it.

We've all had the experience—a blend of aroma, sounds, tastes, textures, and colors—that transport us back in time to when food was so formative and familiar; to the kitchens and dining rooms and back decks of our childhoods; where dishes were prepared while we curiously watched. Mixing bowls spun, pots simmered, and grill lids were lifted high—setting free billowing clouds of fragrant smoke.

These memories are the wells from which we draw our identities. They give meaning to the stories we tell. We use them to connect with ourselves. It's no surprise that we use them to connect with each other—everyone can talk about food, family, and home.

FOOD

Few topics can warm up an interview with a country music star faster than talking about food. I've certainly heard some wonderful food tales in writing this book. Not many get simpler than those of William Lee Golden of The Oak Ridge Boys. He'll forsake all things gastronomical—the finest cuts of meat, the most exotic fruits—for a good jar of peanut butter. His dad was a peanut farmer in South Alabama, and that creamy spread scooped straight out with a spoon taps memories of mud-caked work boots, wide-brimmed hats, and sweat-stained shirts; of his mother's hands methodically making peanut butter sandwiches. William Lee also remembers how his mother baked scrumptious desserts, and that she passed her skills down to his sister Lanette, who has now become notorious for making an Orange Dreamsicle Cake (page 208) that regularly appears at Golden family gatherings.

Sharing skills and cooking techniques turned out to be the way singer-songwriter Sarah Darling fell in love with an Englishman. Thousands of miles and an ocean separated Sarah from her beau, James Muriel, so the two cultivated their relationship using Skype, the real-time webcam software, to cook dinner together. They learned the other's likes and dislikes. They experimented with foreign flavors. Through the video feed on their computer screens, they created romantic evenings making food, despite the distance. Now they are married, live in Nashville, and still love to share recipes. James has taught Sarah how to make the English dessert banoffee pie. Sarah, in turn, has shown James how to make her Grandma Alice's Pumpkin Bars (page 71).

> **FEW TOPICS CAN WARM UP AN INTERVIEW WITH A COUNTRY MUSIC STAR FASTER THAN TALKING ABOUT FOOD. I'VE CERTAINLY HEARD SOME WONDERFUL FOOD TALES IN WRITING THIS BOOK.**

"THROUGH GOOD AND BAD TIMES FOOD WAS ALWAYS WHAT BOUND US TOGETHER."

FAMILY

Wynonna Judd says hers is a family of strong personalities that disagree about nearly everything. At the dinner table, though, rules are rules and mealtimes are sacred. Her mother Naomi long ago established the rule that no matter what is happening in the world, the table is a place of peace. That's a lesson she is teaching her daughter Grace, whom she is also showing how to make a broccoli casserole recipe (page 166) that's been in the family for years.

In addition to recipes, families often pass down kitchen wares, which is the case for Amy Grant and her husband Vince Gill. Amy always pulls a blue speckled roasting pan from her pantry when she makes her family-favorite Amy's Pot Roast

(page 136). The pan bears special significance because it belonged to her husband Vince's grandmother. Amy has so much respect for the woman that she was inspired to perfect her own pot roast recipe so she could use the pan.

For singer Kree Harrison, her Mom's Gumbo (page 142) or fried shrimp always reminds her of her parents. Her mother was a great cook who was influenced by Cajun dishes, and she made gumbo for Christmas each year. Her father always prided himself on the special seasoning he concocted for his shrimp batter. These foods have become touchstones for Kree, ways to help her remember her parents, who passed too soon.

THE
SECOND
FIDDLE

MUSIC
HONKY TONK
CITY

WELCOME TO
LAYLA'S
BLUEGRASS INN
NASHVILLE

Second
Fiddle

ATM

Bud

HOME

One line plumbs the entire book. It's the love of the road, the frenzied fame and all it affords juxtaposed with the longing for home and the respite and equanimity home provides. These folks don't roll with kitchens. They live with catering. They fit coolers into the corners of the tour bus.

Over and over again, artists spoke about how making a meal was deeply grounding, and how cooking is an entry point for returning to normalcy, to home base.

CMT host Allison DeMarcus says her husband Jay commands the kitchen when he comes off the road with his group Rascal Flatts. They are both able to unwind by creating pasta dishes and Miss Caron's Pizza Casserole (page 90) from his mother's recipes. The dishes are fun for the family and an homage to his Italian heritage.

Singer-songwriter Holly Williams (Hank, Jr.'s daughter) says that cooking is her therapy. When she's tired, she would rather invite friends over and cook for them—something light like Beach House Pasta (230) or sweet like Melting Moments (page 233)—than crash on her couch. She loves her kitchen, which she designed to be open and accessible, because it invigorates her.

And then there's teenage singer Scotty McCreery, who lives on his own but is still his mother's boy in so many ways. She is just as happy to serve his favorites—fried chicken, green beans, mashed potatoes, and Grandma Janet's Broccoli Cornbread (page 186)—as he is to eat them while he's back home sharing the details of his touring travels.

This book gives you a glimpse at the genuine lives of these country stars. You might be surprised, like I was, at how familiar the anecdotes sound.

Like Miranda Lambert, we crave the comfort foods our mothers taught us how to make. Like Craig Morgan, we savor the produce pulled straight from our gardens. Like Laura Bell Bundy, we add a little "kick" to our marinades.

The truth is that most of us thumb through well-worn, passed-down recipes on special occasions. We rely on the rhythm of holiday traditions. And we've sworn oaths to guard the family's secret sauce ingredient.

Granted, very few of us have performed before thousands, but who hasn't popped in a table leaf to welcome an extra three?

You'll cook wonderful dishes using the recipes on these pages, but in the bigger sense, you'll be reminded of how we all connect with kindred stories when it comes to food, family, and home.

—Tanner Latham

FEATU

A → C

JRING

D → F

Trace Adkins

Trace Adkins has traveled a long way from the small Louisiana town where he was raised and the gospel quartet that gave him his voice. But no matter how much fame this superstar gains, Trace stays true to himself.

If you look closely at Trace Adkins's left pinky finger, you'll notice it sits at an odd, 90-degree angle. Back before he was the internationally known singer-songwriter who has sold more than 10 million albums or the television personality who charmed Donald Trump on *All-Star Celebrity Apprentice*, Trace was a roughneck on an oil rig. He cut his pinky clean off in a gruesome accident, and when the doctors reattached it, they couldn't set it correctly.

Trace is honest about his limitations. "There are a lot of chords that I just simply can't make anymore," he has said about playing guitar with his bum finger. "So I do the best I can." But this hasn't slowed him any.

He grew up in Sarepta, Louisiana, a tiny town that sits way up in the northwestern corner of the state, not too far from Arkansas and Texas. The population hovers around 1,000 people, and a welcome sign touts their most famous and favorite son: Home of Trace Adkins.

"I had a Norman Rockwell-style Southern childhood in small-town America," he writes in his 2007 autobiography, *A Personal Stand: Observations and Opinions from a Freethinking Roughneck*. "My paternal grandparents lived about a mile and a half from my home, while the maternal pair lived about 3 miles away. We were always there for each other in our peaceful, God-fearing town. It felt secure to be a kid with both sets of grandparents and lots of kinfolk close by whenever I needed them."

The young man lived to be outdoors, but he also developed an ear for music, learning to play guitar and sing at an early age. Trace's mother and aunts sang in the choir at the Baptist church in town, and when he was in high school, Trace joined a gospel group called the New Commitment Quartet. They recorded a couple of albums and performed in the area.

"I think having sung gospel music was the most valuable thing," Trace has said. "I learned more about music in the five years that I sang bass in the gospel quartet than any other time." Trace was also musically inspired by classic country artists, such as Merle Haggard and Ronnie Milsap, as well as classic rock bands, including Lynyrd Skynyrd, Journey, and the Eagles. In the early 1990s he started playing small stages in Nashville, and as the story goes, a Capitol Records executive saw him perform and signed him, and Trace's career rocketed.

After almost 20 years as a mainstay on the country scene, Trace is the proud father of five daughters and the happy husband to his wife, Rhonda, to whom he proposed on the Grand Ole Opry stage the night he was inducted. On the rare days when the family is home and settled, they like a nice, simple meal—something along the lines of the classic Poppy Seed Chicken Casserole, which everyone enjoys.

Trace still produces music spanning a wide spectrum. It can be as sentimental as "You're Gonna Miss This" and as suggestive as "Honky Tonk Badonkadonk." What you can count on, as sure as that permanently bent pinky finger, is that Trace will be Trace. Honestly.

albums & awards

Academy of Country Music, Top New Male Vocalist, 1996

CMT Awards, Male Video of the Year for "I Got My Game On," 2008

Academy of Country Music, Single of the Year for "You're Gonna Miss This," 2009

CMT Awards for Collaborative Video of the Year, "Hillbilly Bone" with Blake Shelton, 2010

Academy of Country Music, Vocal Event of the Year, "Hillbilly Bone" with Blake Shelton, 2010

TRACE ADKINS
Greatest Hits Collection, Volume I

Trace Adkins has sold more than 10 million albums.

BEING THE PARENTS OF FIVE MEANS MEALS ARE HECTIC AND FUN, SO **TRACE AND HIS WIFE, RHONDA, KEEP IT SIMPLE.**

POPPY SEED CHICKEN CASSEROLE

**makes: 8 to 10 servings   hands-on time: 20 min.
total time: 1 hour, 15 min.**

The Adkins crew likes to serve this classic casserole for supper with rice, green beans, and dinner rolls.

4	(6-oz.) boneless chicken breasts, cooked and cubed
1	(16-oz.) container sour cream
1	(10 ³/₄-oz.) can cream of chicken soup, undiluted
1	(10 ³/₄-oz.) can cream of mushroom soup, undiluted
¹/₄	tsp. table salt
¹/₂	tsp. freshly ground black pepper
2	rolls round buttery crackers (about 70), crushed
¹/₂	cup butter or margarine, melted
1	Tbsp. poppy seeds

1. Preheat oven to 350°. Place cooked cubed chicken in bottom of a lightly greased 11- x 7-inch baking dish.

2. Whisk together sour cream, soups, salt, and pepper in a medium bowl; spread over chicken.

3. Stir together crushed crackers, melted butter, and poppy seeds. Sprinkle over top of soup mixture.

4. Bake at 350° for 30 to 45 minutes or until bubbly.

☛ TIP ☚

It's a great idea to crush crackers in a large zip-top plastic bag. Use your rolling pin for quick, even results.

TRACE AND RHONDA'S DAUGHTER, BRIANNA, LOVES THESE EASY COOKIES. **THEY ARE PERFECT TO MAKE** WHEN IT'S TOO DARN HOT TO TURN ON THE OVEN!**"**

NO-BAKE COCOA COOKIES

**makes: about 4 dozen   hands-on time: 30 min.
total time: 1 hour, 5 min.**

2   cups sugar
¼   cup unsweetened cocoa
¼   cup corn oil
½   cup soy milk

2   tsp. vanilla extract
2½ cups uncooked quick-cooking
      oats

1. Whisk together sugar, cocoa, oil, and milk in a heavy saucepan. Cook over medium heat until boiling, stirring occasionally. Boil exactly 1 minute. (If you cook more than 1 minute, the balls will be too hard.)

2. Remove from heat. Add vanilla extract and quick oats, stirring well. Let stand 2 to 3 minutes.

3. Scoop mixture into 1-inch balls, and drop onto lightly greased wax paper. Cool thoroughly.

★ ★ ★

These simple drop cookies are a sweet treat for kids with dairy or wheat allergies.

★ ★ ★

☛ **TIP** ☚

To avoid getting burned, make sure to wait 2 to 3 minutes before scooping the hot mixture into balls.

Lauren Alaina

Lauren Alaina grew up singing wherever she could find a stage—from churches to restaurants and karaoke bars. Though still a teenager, this American Idol *star is a success on the country stage.*

Growing up, Lauren Alaina Kristine Suddeth was the baby of her family. When it came to cooking for big events like Thanksgiving and Christmas, the older women—her aunt, grandmother, and mother, particularly—often nudged her out of the kitchen. So she made herself useful in another way— she seized the opportunity to sing. "I was the entertainment while everyone else worked," she recalls.

Singing has been a part of Lauren's life as long as she can remember. Both her mother, Kristy, and brother, Tyler, sang, and her father, J.J., played several instruments. Lauren sang in churches and restaurants and says she would seek out karaoke anywhere within a 30-mile radius of where she lived. That was Rossville, Georgia, a small town right on the state's northern border about 5 miles from Chattanooga, Tennessee.

Lauren idolized Shania Twain, and her mother tells the story that, when Lauren was 3 years old, they were listening to the Dixie Chicks singing "You Were Mine" on the radio. After her mother turned the car off, Lauren kept on singing the song, word for word, note for note. At age 16, she landed a spot on the show *American Idol*—and shortened her name to Lauren Alaina. After surviving the entire season, singing songs by Shania and Martina McBride and Lee Ann Womack, she was declared runner-up. That launched her career, and her first album, *Wildflower*, which is full of high-energy, spunky songs mixed with a few slower ballads, sold almost 70,000 copies its first week.

The singer's family is starting to detect hints of a culinary breakthrough as well. Her grandmother

albums & awards

Lauren Alaina's first album, *Wildflower*, featured the single "Georgia Peaches" and sold close to 70,000 copies in its first week.

In 2012, Lauren won the American Country Award for New Artist of the Year.

Her recent singles include "Eighteen Inches" (2012) and "Barefoot and Buckwild" (2013).

Lauren's musical break came at age 16 when she was the runner-up in the 10th season of American Idol.

Linda Suddeth has started asking if Lauren wants to come over and help her cook. "I'm thinking, 'Wow, I'm allowed in the kitchen!' I have a feeling it's going to be a trap, though," Lauren says with a laugh. "They'll teach me their tricks, and I'll have to do all the cooking!"

Apparently, just about everyone in Lauren's family can cook, so learning the craft from them is akin to professional training. Grandmother Suddeth ("She makes the best homemade biscuits!") once owned a restaurant. Her aunt Christie Suddeth ("She makes the best homemade cheesecake!") once had a cafe nestled in a strip mall in East Ridge, Tennessee, outside Chattanooga. During Lauren's *American Idol* run, you could find a makeshift shrine of support—a collage of headshots and news clippings—in one of the cafe's corners. Christie eventually sold the restaurant, but Lauren's cousin Jake Suddeth, a longtime cook, still mans the grill.

With her music career taking off, Lauren's on the road a great deal, so she really appreciates coming home to her mother's meatloaf, mashed potatoes, and macaroni and cheese. "She hooks me up!" says Lauren.

Lauren adds that she's now living on her own in her first apartment—and that's motivation enough to take her grandmother Suddeth up on her offer to join her in the kitchen. If there's one thing Lauren would like to master, it's her grandmother's Blackberry Cobbler. "I'm obsessed with it," she says. When she was little, her grandmother always prepared the cobbler when Lauren came to visit. She says it's a recipe that's been passed down for several generations.

"AS A LITTLE GIRL, I REMEMBER ALWAYS WANTING MY GRANDMOTHER TO MAKE BLACKBERRY COBBLER FOR ME."

BLACKBERRY COBBLER

makes: 4 to 6 servings   hands-on time: 15 min.
total time: 1 hour, 35 min.

★ ★ ★

Simple and simply delicious, this cobbler comes from Lauren's grandmother Linda Suddeth, who owned a restaurant for several years.

★ ★ ★

2½ cups fresh or frozen blackberries, thawed and drained
1 cup sugar
1 cup all-purpose flour
2 tsp. baking powder
½ tsp. table salt
1 cup milk
½ cup butter, melted
½ tsp. ground cinnamon
Whipped cream or ice cream

1. Preheat oven to 375°. Stir together blackberries and sugar in a medium bowl. Let stand about 20 minutes or until fruit syrup forms.

2. Whisk together flour, baking powder, salt, and milk in another medium bowl. Stir in melted butter until blended. Spread batter in an ungreased 8-inch square baking pan. Spoon blackberry mixture over batter. Sprinkle with cinnamon.

3. Bake at 375° for 45 minutes or until puffed and golden. Serve warm with whipped cream or ice cream. Sprinkle with additional ground cinnamon.

 TIP

If you are using frozen berries, thaw them in a sieve over a bowl to catch the juice.

Cody Alan

CMT television and radio personality Cody Alan has been in the business since he was a teenager. Get to know him just a little, and you'll see exactly why.

Once Cody Alan starts talking about his favorite on-air interview moments, it's a bit difficult to get him to stop. Like the time when he gave Taylor Swift a slow cooker as a housewarming gift, and she was as grateful as if he had handed her a Grammy. Or when Kenny Chesney admitted in public that he cried during the movie *Forrest Gump*. Or when Cody, who loves wearing Converse Chuck Taylor All Star shoes, gave Blake Shelton, who thinks Chuck Taylors are silly, a pair. "He says they look like 'clown shoes,' and he always called me the Converse Cowboy," Cody laughs, remembering that exchange. "It was hilarious!"

These stories are fun, yes. But they also illustrate how people, especially country music stars, respond so positively to Cody's genuineness. With his signature black ball cap and infectious smile, he brings levity to any situation.

"I always try to have fun with the artist and make them laugh," he says. "Beyond that, I want to have an emotional connection. As a host, I try to be like a great waiter at a restaurant. I want to get you the entrée you came for and yet enhance your overall experience with knowledge and a smile." It's a gift he has used his whole life.

Cody grew up with country music. His mother played it on their kitchen radio every morning while she was cooking breakfast, and his father introduced him to the classic country performers, including Dolly Parton and Kenny Rogers. At 8 years old, Cody decided that radio would be his path. "I knew I wanted to draw pictures in people's minds," he remarks.

awards

Cody Alan received the Academy of Country Music Award for National On-Air Personality of the Year in 2010 and 2013.

In 2012, Cody was named one of *Nashville Lifestyles* magazine's 25 Most Beautiful People.

Cody can be heard daily on *CMT Radio Live with Cody Alan* and can be seen on CMT's *Hot 20 Countdown* music video and interview show as well as CMT's *#1 Music and a Movie.*

Cody began working at country music radio station WCOS in Columbia, South Carolina, when he was in high school. He made his "on-air" debut when he was 15 years old.

When he was in high school, he interned at country music station WCOS. Eventually an on-air host got sick on a Sunday graveyard shift, and Cody was called. "It was my big chance!" he exclaims. He was 15 years old and on the air, living his dream. Soon the station gave him regular shifts. "I was that young and already doing what I thought I was born to do," he says. "It was the only thing that made me cool in high school."

Twenty years later, Cody hosts his own CMT radio shows, *Live with Cody Alan* and *After MidNite!* But you don't just hear Cody. You can also see him on CMT's shows *Hot 20 Countdown* and *#1 Music and a Movie.*

With these gigs, sometimes it's a challenge to find time to be home. It's no surprise that Sundays have become the big meal days for the family. "Meals give you that chance to sit down, relax, and talk to each other," he says. "Those are times to have easy conversations, enjoy each other's company, and build real relationships with your children."

On those days, they love to make Sunday Chicken, a creamy slow-cooker recipe his mother gave him when he moved out of his family home at age 18. It's simple and tasty, and he's taught his kids how to make it. Taco Soup has become another family favorite, especially when paired with Jalapeño Cheese Cornbread. "We really like to light up the taste buds, Mexican style!" Cody says with a laugh.

Like the chicken, the taco soup is another simple, hearty slow-cooker recipe that can last as leftovers for a few days. And, yes, there's a slow-cooker theme with Cody. He really loves cooking with it because he believes it's just so useful. Apparently Taylor Swift agrees.

TACO SOUP HAS BECOME AN ALAN FAMILY FAVORITE, ESPECIALLY WHEN PAIRED WITH JALAPEÑO CHEESE CORNBREAD. **"WE REALLY LIKE TO LIGHT UP THE TASTE BUDS, MEXICAN STYLE!"**

TACO SOUP

makes: 14 cups   hands-on time: 20 min.
total time: 55 min.

Taco Soup makes a great go-to recipe for an easy night of entertaining friends or a quick weeknight supper for your family. Most of the ingredients are pantry staples, so you'll be able to put it together quickly.

1 lb. ground beef
2 (16-oz.) cans pinto beans, drained and rinsed
1 (16-oz.) package frozen cut green beans
1 (15-oz.) can ranch beans, undrained
1 (14.5-oz.) can stewed tomatoes
1 (14.5-oz.) can petite diced tomatoes, undrained
1 (12-oz.) package frozen whole kernel corn
1 (12-oz.) bottle beer*
1 (1-oz.) envelope taco seasoning mix
1 (1-oz.) envelope Ranch dressing mix

Toppings: tortilla strips, shredded Cheddar cheese, sliced green onions

1. Brown beef in a large Dutch oven over medium-high heat, stirring constantly, 8 to 10 minutes or until meat crumbles and is no longer pink; drain. Return to Dutch oven.

2. Stir pinto beans, next 8 ingredients, and 2 cups water into beef; bring to a boil.

3. Reduce heat to medium-low. Simmer, stirring occasionally, 30 minutes. Serve with desired toppings.

*1½ cups chicken broth may be substituted.

CODY HOSTS RADIO AND TV SHOWS SO HIS SUNDAYS ARE PRECIOUS TIME RESERVED FOR HIS FAMILY. "WE ENJOY EACH OTHER'S COMPANY."

SUNDAY CHICKEN

makes: 4 servings   hands-on time: 20 min.
total time: 3 hours, 20 min.

2   boneless chicken breasts
4   slices bacon (the old-fashioned, uncooked kind)
Table salt to taste
Freshly ground black pepper to taste

1   (10 ¾-oz.) can cream of chicken soup
2   cups sour cream
1   (14-oz.) can chicken broth

1. Wash chicken. Wrap each chicken breast with 2 pieces of bacon, and sprinkle with salt and pepper. Place chicken in a slow cooker.

2. Mix the soup and sour cream together, and spread on chicken. Pour broth over top.

3. Cook on HIGH 3 to 4 hours or until desired degree of doneness.

★ ★ ★

This simple slow-cooker supper practically prepares itself, leaving you free to enjoy the day.

★ ★ ★

JALAPEÑO CHEESE CORNBREAD

makes: 1 loaf   hands-on time: 27 min.
total time: 53 min.

1   (15-oz.) box Krusteaz Natural Honey Cornbread & Muffin Mix
½   cup grated Cheddar cheese

2   Tbsp. diced jalapeño peppers
1   cup creamed corn (optional)

1. Preheat oven to 400°. Prepare cornbread mix in a medium mixing bowl according to package instructions.

2. Stir cheese and jalapeños into cornbread mix. Add creamed corn, if desired.

3. Pour cornbread mixture into a lightly greased 8-inch or 9-inch baking dish. Bake at 400° for 22 to 26 minutes or until golden brown.

Laura Bell Bundy

Wherever you find her—on stages from Broadway to Nashville, at a Wildcat game, or in front of the stove—this Kentucky girl turned showstopping star brings her special spark.

There's no denying the feisty spirit of singer-songwriter and actress Laura Bell Bundy. You can hear it in her music, especially on upbeat songs such as "Giddy On Up" and "I'm No Good (For Ya Baby)," in which she takes a stand or confronts a man. "I believe my music should be fun," she says. "It should be a party...a danceable, fun, flirty, joyful party." You can see it on stage when her spark and charisma corral the audience.

It all makes sense, considering Laura Bell (yes, she goes by both names and even answers to the initials LBB) has been performing her whole life. At nine, she debuted on stage in the *Radio City Christmas Spectacular.* The next year, she starred in the off-Broadway production of *Ruthless, The Musical,* earning an Outer Critics Circle Award nomination and Theatre World Award for her role. By age 14, she was writing her own country songs, and four years later, she formed her own band.

As an adult, acting was the path Laura Bell first truly followed. She starred in several Broadway shows, including *Hairspray, Legally Blonde: The Musical* (for which she received a Tony nomination), and *Wicked.* You also might have seen her in several movies and television series, most notably *Jumanji, Dreamgirls, Guiding Light, Cold Case,* and *How I Met Your Mother.*

In 2008, Laura Bell shifted her focus to country music when she moved to Nashville. She had grown up idolizing Dolly Parton and Reba McEntire. "They were both all about storytelling," she explains. "Storytelling connects, and when you add music to it, all the emotions are heightened." The album she released in 2010, *Achin' and Shakin',* reached number five on the country charts.

These days, her career straddles both music and acting. She recently landed a leading role in the television series *Anger Management,* which stars

Singer-songwriter and actress Laura Bell Bundy has starred in several Broadway shows, including *Hairspray, Legally Blonde: The Musical,* and *Wicked.*

Charlie Sheen. She also just released the hard-rockin' "Two Step" and "Kentucky Dirty," which pays homage to her home state of Kentucky and the University of Kentucky basketball team.

Laura Bell grew up in Lexington, Kentucky, where food was big, especially during sporting events. Her relatives have always been huge University of Kentucky basketball fans. "When there's a game, we get nervous, and it's like we're all standing around the counter hovering," she says, adding that they make a lot of dips, including homemade Ranch dressing, chili cheese dip, and a beer cheese dip recipe Laura Bell has sworn to keep secret. Beer cheese, a spicy cheese spread, is very popular in Kentucky. "This should be big in Wisconsin, but they don't have anything that tastes as good as ours," she emphasizes.

Laura Bell wears her Kentucky pride on her sleeve, sometimes literally. "If you don't get a UK T-shirt for Christmas, something is amiss," she says. This has always been the case—during her years as a Broadway actress in New York as well as now that she's splitting her time between Nashville and Los Angeles. She's still a girl from Kentucky. She loves basketball, bluegrass, horses, beer cheese, and bourbon, an ingredient she likes to use as a meat tenderizer.

Laura Bell traces her love of cooking to an old family recipe for shepherd's pie. She figures she was just 10 years old when she first learned to make it. Her grandmother and her ancestors were Irish, and the recipe was a family favorite, passed down from generation to generation. She spent lots of time in the kitchen observing and watching her mother. "She was my teacher even without realizing it," she notes. This was the case with the shepherd's pie, but Laura Bell never needed to write down the recipe. "The truth is that I know this recipe by heart."

(continued on page 37)

> **PERFORMING THROUGHOUT MY LIFE HAS INFLUENCED HOW I WANT TO SHARE MY MUSIC WITH THE WORLD. I BELIEVE MY MUSIC SHOULD BE FUN. IT SHOULD BE A PARTY...A DANCEABLE, FUN, FLIRTY, JOYFUL PARTY.**

Cooking skills became even more important when, at age 20, Laura Bell was diagnosed with celiac disease. "This was way before gluten free was cool," she notes. At that point, it was difficult to find gluten-free products in grocery stores or on restaurant menus. "I had to start really cooking to eat the things I wanted to," she recalls. "I started to eat at home at lot because it was easier." Fortunately, she never lost the interest in cooking that began when she was a girl. "There's something so therapeutic about making meals, and I've discovered new things because I've had to be experimental."

When Laura Bell spends time at home or with her boyfriend, she enjoys making gluten-free pasta and homemade sauces, such as meaty Bolognese, herbaceous pesto, and her own Gluten-Free Spaghetti Pomodoro. She says they are "total foodies." One of her favorite Italian restaurants in New York served a version of this dish, and she taught herself how to make it.

As you might expect, the spunk, fire, and independence Laura Bell exhibits on stage also come through in the kitchen. "I'm not a good recipe follower," she notes. "I usually like to go with my gut when it comes to cooking."

The album art for Longing for a Place Already Gone is bursting with personality just like Laura Bell.

albums & awards

Laura Bell has acted in several movies and television series, most notably *Jumanji, Dreamgirls, Guiding Light, Cold Case,* and *How I Met Your Mother.*

She received a Tony nomination in the Best Performance by a Leading Actress category for playing the role of Elle Woods in *Legally Blonde: The Musical,* 2007

She released her first album, *Longing for a Place Already Gone,* in 2007.

Laura Bell's second album, *Achin' and Shakin',* reached number five on the country charts.

LAURA BELL SPLITS HER TIME BETWEEN NASHVILLE AND LOS ANGELES, BUT SHE'LL ALWAYS BE A GIRL FROM KENTUCKY.

"THERE'S SOMETHING SO THERAPEUTIC ABOUT MAKING MEALS, AND I'VE DISCOVERED NEW THINGS BECAUSE I'VE HAD TO BE EXPERIMENTAL. I'M NOT A GOOD RECIPE FOLLOWER. I COOK FOR TASTE."

★ ★ ★

After being diagnosed with celiac disease, Laura Bell Bundy had to be careful about what she ate. So she asked chefs at Italian restaurants how to make their amazing sauces. This one was a simple sauce she developed through trial and error.

★ ★ ★

GLUTEN-FREE SPAGHETTI POMODORO

makes: 4 servings   hands-on time: 15 min.   total time: 50 min.

1 (12-oz.) package gluten-free spaghetti	½ cup chopped fresh basil
2 Tbsp. minced garlic	Table salt
¼ cup olive oil	Freshly ground black pepper
1 (26.46 oz.) carton baby chopped tomatoes	

1. Cook pasta according to package directions. (All gluten-free pastas cook a little differently, so make sure to read the directions.)

2. Cook garlic in hot oil in a large nonstick skillet over medium heat 1 minute. Add tomatoes; cook 2 to 3 minutes. Stir in basil; simmer on low heat 15 minutes. Add salt and pepper to taste.

3. Combine sauce and pasta. Serve immediately.

NOTE: We tested with Tinkyáda Pasta Joy Organic Brown Rice Spaghetti and Pomi Chopped Tomatoes.

Craig Campbell

South Georgia native Craig Campbell rarely strays far from the themes of love, home, and family in his music. The singer-songwriter sets those as priorities in his life as well.

Craig Campbell is prejudiced when it comes to onions. For him, it's Vidalias or nothing else. "Regular onions don't taste as good to me," he says. No wonder. The singer-songwriter, known best for his neo-traditional style (more twang, less bling) and for playing piano and guitar in his songs—grew up outside Lyons, Georgia, 5 miles from the city of Vidalia, where daily helpings of the famous local sweet onions are the norm.

Craig says his family grew a lot of what they ate. His stepfather had a green thumb and maintained a year-round garden with bounteous rows of corn, okra, cucumbers, peas, squash, mustard greens, and collard greens. "When I was a kid, I didn't like it," recalls Craig. He had to pick, wash, and shell whatever they were harvesting. "I thought it was terrible, but it made for good character."

They also raised hogs and hunted deer during the season, and Craig says his mother knew exactly what to do with all that food. "Everything my momma made was awesome," he says. She fried cornbread thin enough to see through, a perfect pairing for a mess of mustard greens. "And her mashed potatoes were like heaven."

Craig says his mother also practiced a spirit of inclusiveness. After hosting big family dinners at holidays and after-Sunday-church gatherings, she grew tired of the kids and grandkids stealing off to different rooms to dine. So she had a massive dinner table custom built. Her table still is big enough to accommodate everyone.

Craig doesn't get back to that table and those family dinners as often as he wants these days. He moved to Nashville more than a decade ago and played keyboards in the bands of country artists Tracy Byrd and Luke Bryan. After being discovered while singing at one of the city's honky-tonks, The Stage on Broadway, he recorded two solo albums and now spends lots of time on the road.

When he does have the chance to visit his family's place in Georgia, he often stocks up on bags of Vidalias to cook and share back in Eagleville, Tennessee, where he lives with his wife, Mindy, and their daughters, Preslee and Kinni Rose. Some of those onions make it to his friends. And some of them find their way into his and his wife's favorite dishes, such as Red-Wine Braised Beef Short Ribs and Mashed Potatoes with Caramelized Vidalia Onions.

albums

Craig points to country legends Clint Black and Alan Jackson as great influences on his music.

Singer-songwriter Craig Campbell released the single "Family Man" in 2010, and it reached number 14 on the Billboard Hot Country Songs chart.

His second studio album, *Never Regret*, features a song called "When She Grows Up," inspired by his two young daughters, Preslee and Kinni Rose.

Craig played keyboards for Tracy Byrd and Luke Bryan until he was discovered in Nashville honky-tonk The Stage on Broadway.

COUNTRY MUSIC'S GREATEST EATS

"EVERYTHING MY MAMA MADE WAS AWESOME. SHE FRIED CORNBREAD THIN ENOUGH TO SEE THROUGH, A PERFECT PAIRING FOR A MESS OF MUSTARD GREENS."

RED-WINE BRAISED BEEF SHORT RIBS

**makes: 6 servings   hands-on time: 40 min.
total time: 3 hours, 15 min.**

★ ★ ★

Craig notes that the wine and long, slow cooking are key when preparing this family-favorite dish. When it's done right, he says the meat falls off the bone.

★ ★ ★

6	(5-inch-long) beef short ribs (about 3½ lbs.)
½	tsp. table salt
1	tsp. freshly ground black pepper
2	Tbsp. canola oil
2	cups chopped Vidalia onions
1½	cups chopped carrots
2	(8-oz.) packages baby portabella mushrooms, quartered
3	Tbsp. all-purpose flour
2	cups reduced-sodium beef broth
2	cups dry red wine
1	Tbsp. tomato paste
4	(5-inch) sprigs fresh rosemary
3	to 4 sprigs fresh thyme
1	bay leaf

Garnish: fresh rosemary and thyme sprigs

1. Preheat oven to 325°. Sprinkle short ribs with salt and pepper. Cook ribs in hot oil in a large Dutch oven over medium-high heat 10 minutes or until browned on all sides. Remove ribs; set aside.

2. Reduce heat to medium, and cook onions, carrots, and mushrooms in pan drippings 5 to 10 minutes or until mushrooms have released their liquid. Sprinkle vegetables with flour, and cook, stirring constantly, until mixture is smooth. Stir in beef broth and next 5 ingredients. Cook over medium-high heat, stirring often, 10 minutes or until mixture is reduced by half.

3. Add short ribs to Dutch oven; spoon vegetable mixture over ribs. Cover and bake at 325° for 2 hours and 15 minutes or until meat is tender. Remove rosemary and thyme sprigs and bay leaf before serving.

MASHED POTATOES WITH CARAMELIZED VIDALIA ONIONS

makes: 6 to 8 servings   hands-on time: 40 min.
total time: 1 hour, 5 min.

4	lb. Yukon gold potatoes, peeled and quartered*
1	Tbsp. table salt
1	cup unsalted butter, softened
½	cup half-and-half, warmed

1	tsp. or more table salt to taste
½	tsp. or more freshly ground black pepper to taste
	Caramelized Vidalia Onions

1. Bring potatoes, 1 Tbsp. salt, and water to cover to a boil in a large Dutch oven over medium-high heat, and cook 10 minutes or until potatoes are tender. Drain potatoes, return to Dutch oven, and cook over low heat, shaking occasionally, until potatoes are dry. Remove from heat.

2. Add butter to potatoes and mash. Stir in half-and-half; add salt and pepper to taste. Top with Caramelized Vidalia Onions.

*You can also use unpeeled, well-scrubbed young potatoes and mash them with their skins on.

CARAMELIZED VIDALIA ONIONS

makes: 1 cup   hands-on time: 20 min.   total time: 20 min.

1	large Vidalia onion, thinly sliced
2	pinches of brown or white sugar

2	Tbsp. olive oil

1. Cook Vidalia onion slices and sugar in hot oil in a non-stick skillet over medium-high heat 20 minutes, stirring often, until onions are caramel-colored.

★ ★ ★

For Craig, Vidalia onions are a connection to Georgia Vidalia country, where he grew up. If he is using them to garnish meats like steak or as a topping for mashed potatoes, he simply slices them thinly, throws them in a pan with a little olive oil, adds a few pinches of brown sugar to help them caramelize, and cooks them until they're tender.

★ ★ ★

Katie Cook

As a CMT host, Katie Cook spends her days quizzing the stars on their lives, loves, and music. But her weekends are reserved for family, food, and fun.

Longtime CMT host Katie Cook and her daughter, Daisy Rocket (hang on to hear more about that spunky name), have a special Saturday morning ritual. It centers on Fancy Pancakes. Katie pours the pancake batter into different shapes—flowers or peace signs or swirly galaxies or bears—and then uses fruit to create facial features and other details. "It's like a challenge every weekend," says Katie, who often creates the pancakes to suit Daisy's requests. "When she gets specific, I have to work hard to make them happen."

Katie says she's known her whole life that if she ever had a girl, she would name her Daisy. "But it was such a sweet name, and my daughter's name needed a little edge," she explains. She tried a lot of cosmic words and names of planets, and "rocket" got thrown into the mix. "I started trying it out on people, and it—took off," Katie recalls, laughing. "I wish my name was Daisy Rocket!"

The pancake tradition she shares with her daughter is a fun twist on what Katie shared with her own mother. She made Katie's family a hot breakfast—often a stack of raisin pancakes—every morning before school.

Katie was born in England, where her father, Roger Cook, was a singer-songwriter. Roger eventually moved the family to Nashville to continue his successful music career, and he has been inducted into both the Nashville Songwriters Hall of Fame and the Songwriters Hall of Fame. His notable songs include "I'd Like To Teach the World To Sing (In Perfect Harmony)" and "Long Cool Woman in a Black Dress."

"When we moved to Nashville, it was a bizarre thing. My dad was like a fish out of water. He had a Rolls Royce that he brought with us, and he bought a farm in Franklin, Tennessee, which was way in the middle of nowhere then. You can just imagine how strange that Rolls Royce looked driving down the back roads," says Katie.

Katie was 5 years old when her family moved. The family was vegetarian, and Katie remembers her parents' love of Indian food. That served as inspiration when she created her Vegan Massaman Curry with Tofu. "My parents were always asking us how much fruit or vegetables we had eaten that day," she says. Though her mom and dad eventually began eating meat again, Katie never developed a taste for it herself.

She is proud of the fact that she can go into a restaurant, taste something, and identify what ingredients are in it. "I can't wait to go to the store and dream up the flavors," she says. "I love the challenge of cooking, and I think I'm good at it." That's what she did with her Tofu Lettuce Wraps recipe after trying something similar at an Asian restaurant. Some of her favorite vegetarian recipes come directly from her family, such as the Minted Pea Soup her brother, Jason, makes.

She and Jason formed a band called Reno. Then, after pursuing a solo music career for a short while, Katie auditioned for a host position at CMT, and it all came together. Now she's been hosting shows and events for almost 15 years.

That busy career means she doesn't get a chance to cook as much as she wants, but she still manages to make at least one home-cooked meal per day. And like her parents, she's making a lot of Indian cuisine, especially because Daisy Rocket is starting to love curry.

albums

In 2000, Reno released an eponymously named album.

Katie began her career singing with her brother, Jason, in their band Reno.

"EVERY SATURDAY MORNING IS PANCAKE TIME AT OUR HOUSE. I TRY TO SURPRISE MY DAUGHTER, DAISY ROCKET, WITH A DIFFERENT DESIGN EVERY TIME."

FANCY PANCAKES

makes: 4 servings (4 large or 8 small pancakes)
hands-on time: 30 min.
total time: 30 min., including preparing mix

1 ½ cups Pancake Mix
1 Tbsp. sugar
1 ½ cups buttermilk
1 large egg, lightly beaten
1 Tbsp. vegetable oil
Fruit slices, berries, chocolate chips, marshmallows, Cheerios

1. Combine Pancake Mix and sugar in a medium bowl.

2. Whisk together buttermilk, egg and oil; add to pancake mixture, whisking just until dry ingredients are moistened.

3. Pour about ¼ cup batter for each pancake in the shape you want it to be onto a hot, lightly greased griddle or large nonstick skillet.

4. Cook pancakes 2 minutes or until tops are covered with bubbles and edges look cooked; turn and cook 2 more minutes or until done.

5. Add strawberry or banana slices, chocolate chips, marshmallows, or Cheerios to make facial features or decorate the pancakes.

PANCAKE MIX

makes: 6 cups   hands-on time: 10 min.   total time: 10 min.

6 cups all-purpose flour
3 Tbsp. baking powder
2 tsp. baking soda
2 tsp. table salt

1. Stir together all ingredients in a large bowl; store in a zip-top plastic bag up to 6 weeks.

NOTE: Pancake mix and basic pancakes recipe are from *Southern Living* February 2007. Assembly instructions are from Katie Cook.

★ ★ ★

It's easy to make different pancake shapes. For a bear or mouse face, pour a circle, and wait for it to spread out; then spoon in two tiny circles for the ears. For flowers, start with a small circle, and then spoon long strips around the outside. Katie makes peace signs, swirly Milky Way galaxies, and suns, too. Get creative!

★ ★ ★

VEGAN MASSAMAN CURRY WITH TOFU

makes: 8 servings   **hands-on time: 1 hour, 10 min.**
total time: 1 hour, 30 min.

★ ★ ★

Katie grew up eating lots of Indian food prepared by her parents, who were the inspiration for this curry.

★ ★ ★

¾ (14-oz.) block extra-firm tofu, cut into 32 bite-size triangles
3 Tbsp. vegetable oil, divided
1 large yellow onion, sliced
1 (1-inch) piece fresh ginger, minced
5 garlic cloves, minced
2 Tbsp. Asian Sriracha hot chili sauce
½ cup vegetable broth
4¾ Tbsp. lemongrass paste
¼ cup chopped fresh cilantro
3 bay leaves
1 Tbsp. brown sugar
1 Tbsp. cardamom
1 Tbsp. cumin seed
1 Tbsp. turmeric
2 Tbsp. fresh lime juice
1 cup chopped unsalted cashews, divided
2 (14-oz.) cans coconut milk
2 medium-size baking potatoes, peeled and cut into chunks
2 cups uncooked jasmine rice
1 cup chopped tomato
¾ cup medium-size red bell peppers, sliced
¾ cup medium-size orange bell peppers, sliced
Table salt to taste
Freshly ground black pepper to taste
Garnish: fresh cilantro leaves

1. Stir-fry tofu triangles, in batches, in 1½ Tbsp. hot oil in a large nonstick skillet or wok over medium-high heat 2 to 3 minutes or until lightly browned. Remove tofu from skillet; drain well on paper towels.

2. Add remaining 1½ Tbsp. oil, onion slices, and next 3 ingredients to skillet; stir-fry 2 minutes or until onions are tender. Slowly add vegetable broth. Stir in lemongrass, next 7 ingredients, and ½ cup cashews; bring to a light boil over medium heat, and cook 1 minute. Stir in coconut milk. Add potatoes; cover, reduce heat to low, and simmer 15 to 20 minutes or until potatoes are tender.

3. Cook rice according to package directions; set aside.

4. Stir chopped tomato, sliced peppers, tofu, and remaining cashews into potato mixture. Remove and discard bay leaves. Add salt and pepper to taste. Remove sauce from heat; let stand 5 minutes. Serve sauce over cooked rice.

NOTE: We tested with Gourmet Garden Lemon Grass Paste.

MINTED PEA SOUP

makes: 6 to 8 servings **hands-on time: 30 min.**
total time: 50 min.

3 (16-oz.) bags frozen sweet peas
1 large yellow onion, chopped
4 Tbsp. vegetable oil
2 garlic cloves, chopped
1 (32-oz.) box vegetable broth
½ cup loosely packed fresh mint leaves

2 Tbsp. Asian Sriracha hot chili sauce
1½ Tbsp. table salt
2 tsp. freshly ground black pepper
½ cup sour cream or crème fraiche
Garnish: fresh mint sprigs

1. Prepare peas according to package directions; set aside.

2. Cook chopped onion in hot oil in a large Dutch oven over medium heat 5 to 6 minutes or until tender, stirring occasionally. Add garlic, and cook 1 minute. Reduce heat to medium-low, and cook until onion mixture is lightly browned. Add vegetable broth, and cook 1 minute; remove from heat.

3. Stir in peas, mint leaves, chili sauce, salt, and pepper.

4. Process pea mixture, in batches, in a blender or food processor until smooth, stopping to scrape down sides. (You can also use a handheld immersion blender.)

5. Top each serving with sour cream or crème fraiche.

★ ★ ★

This recipe was developed by Katie's brother and former bandmate, Jason, who continues to perform and also works as a vegan chef in Bristol, England.

★ ★ ★

TOFU LETTUCE WRAPS

makes: 4 servings   hands-on time: 35 min.   total time: 35 min.

A memorable meal at an Asian restaurant inspired this light vegetarian dish.

²/₃ cup lite soy sauce, divided
¹/₄ cup sesame oil
¹/₄ cup spicy brown mustard
2   Tbsp. Asian Sriracha hot chili sauce
2   Tbsp. vegetable oil
2   (14-oz.) blocks extra-firm tofu, drained and cut in ¹/₂-inch cubes

1   small onion, diced
¹/₂ (5-oz.) can water chestnuts, drained and chopped
16   iceberg lettuce leaves
Toppings: chopped green onions, fried Chinese noodles

1. Whisk together ¹/₃ cup soy sauce and next 3 ingredients; set aside.

2. Add vegetable oil to a large nonstick skillet or wok. Add tofu and stir-fry over medium-high heat 7 to 8 minutes or until liquid has evaporated and tofu is browned on all sides. Add diced onion and remaining soy sauce, and stir-fry 5 to 6 minutes.

3. Add water chestnuts and ¹/₄ cup of prepared sauce; stir-fry 2 minutes.

4. Spoon about ¹/₄ cup tofu mixture into lettuce leaves; drizzle with remaining sauce. Serve with toppings.

TIP

Before cutting tofu into cubes, wrap it in two paper towels and press until the towels are completely dampened, soaking up as much liquid as you can without breaking any tofu off.

KATIE COOK'S FAMILY WAS VEGETARIAN.
"MY PARENTS WERE ALWAYS ASKING US HOW MANY FRUITS OR VEGETABLES WE'D EATEN THAT DAY."

VEGETARIAN MEXICAN CHILI DIP

**makes: 12 to 14 servings   hands-on time: 15 min.
total time: 55 min.**

2   (8-oz.) packages cream cheese, softened
1   (8.8-oz.) package ready-to-serve Spanish style rice
3   (15-oz.) cans vegetarian chili with beans
1   (8-oz.) package shredded sharp Cheddar cheese
1   cup chopped tomatoes
½   cup chopped green onions
Tortilla chips

1. Preheat oven to 450°. Spread softened cream cheese in the bottom of a lightly greased 13- x 9-inch glass baking dish.

2. Prepare rice according to package directions; spoon evenly over cream cheese. Spoon chili over rice. Top with Cheddar cheese. Bake at 450° for 10 to 15 minutes or until bubbly and cheese melts. Let stand 10 minutes. Top with tomatoes and green onions. Serve with tortilla chips.

NOTE: We tested with Uncle Ben's Spanish Style Ready Rice and Hormel 99% Fat Free Vegetarian Chili With Beans.

★ ★ ★

This is an easy recipe Katie's mother-in-law taught her a few years ago. She always keeps the ingredients on hand because it's such an easy dish to make for last-minute parties.

★ ★ ★

ROLL WITH IT ★ A LITTLE MORE COUNTRY THAN THAT
This Far from Memphis ★ THE WAY LOVE
LOOKS ★ SOMEDAY WHEN I'M OLD ♫ Don't Ask Me About
a Woman ★ ★ ★ I CAN'T LOVE YOU BACK ★ ★ ★
★ A LOT TO LEARN ABOUT LIVIN' ★ Let Alone You ★ ★ ★

THAT'LL MAKE YOU WANNA DRINK ★
LEAVIN' A LONELY TOWN ★ All Over the Road ★ LOVIN' YOU
IS FUN ★ THAT'S GONNA LEAVE A MEMORY ♫ Hearts Drawn in
the Sand ★ DANCE REAL SLOW ★ A THING FOR YOU
★ ★ ★ Are You With Me ★ ★ THIS FEELS A LOT
LIKE LOVE ★ ★ ★ ONLY A GIRL ★ Tulsa Texas ♫

Easton Corbin

North Central Florida native Easton Corbin has followed a familiar path for country musicians. He was a boy from rural beginnings with a dream and the drive to do whatever it took to take the stage in Nashville.

Easton Corbin's place in Nashville is a total bachelor pad. "I sure don't do a lot of cooking," he says. "And when you look around, you see all my deer heads on the wall." In fact, that's just about all this singer-songwriter needs to make it feel like home. He grew up fishing and hunting, spending lots of time with his grandparents on their cattle farm in small, rural Gilchrist County, west of Gainesville, Florida.

That's where he developed a love for his grandmother's country-fried venison steak. After mincing the meat, she soaked it overnight in buttermilk before battering it and pan-frying it. "It seemed like a big event just to get it together," Easton recalls, adding that once it was salted and peppered, "it melted in your mouth. I know it sounds like a regular country-fried steak, but I'm telling you it's better."

His grandmother cooked a lot during the holidays and was careful to accommodate Easton's and his cousins' requests. They liked her cornbread dressing, minus the onions, so there was always an onion-free dressing on the side. He says she also had a gift for baking, particularly her Coconut Cake with fluffy white frosting that she made from scratch. "Nobody can make it like her," he says.

After high school, Easton attended nearby University of Florida and earned an agribusiness degree. But his dream was to sing and play his guitar, so he moved to Nashville when he was in his mid-twenties. The music life was tough, and he worked in a hardware store during the day and performed nights and weekends at small venues throughout the city.

He finally got a break in 2009 and signed a record deal. His 2010 self-titled debut album included two number one hit singles released the previous year, and fans lauded him as the New/Breakthrough Artist of the Year at the 2010 American Country Awards.

Easton's career has continued to blossom, and he's on the road touring about 200 days per year. Occasionally, he gets back to North Central Florida to visit his family. His stepmother, Debbie Corbin, knows how much he loves her Baby Back Ribs, so when he's home, she makes them, complete with a sweet, homemade sauce.

albums & awards

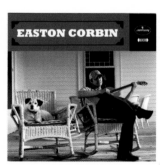

Easton's first two singles, "A Little More Country Than That" and "Roll With It" were number one hits in 2009.

In 2010, he released his self-titled debut album, was named Top New Country Artist by Billboard, and won American Country Awards for New/Breakthrough Artist of the Year and Single by New/Breakthrough Artist of the Year.

Easton cut his teeth touring with big country acts such as Rascal Flatts, Brad Paisley, and Blake Shelton.

GRANDMA'S COCONUT CAKE

makes: 10 to 12 servings   hands-on time: 40 min.
total time: 2 hours, 20 min., including frosting

2	whole eggs	1	Tbsp. baking powder
4	egg yolks	1	cup milk
1½	cups sugar	1	tsp. vanilla extract
½	cup unsalted butter, softened		Fluffy White Frosting
2½	cups cake flour	2	cups shredded fresh coconut

1. Preheat oven to 350°. Beat eggs, egg yolks, and sugar at medium speed with an electric mixer until creamy. Add butter, beating until smooth and creamy.

2. Combine flour and baking powder in a medium bowl; add to egg mixture alternately with milk, beginning and ending with flour mixture. Beat at low speed just until blended after each addition, stopping to scrape bowl as needed. Stir in vanilla.

3. Pour batter into 3 greased and floured 9-inch round cake pans. Bake at 350° for 12 to 13 minutes or until a wooden pick inserted in center comes out clean. Cool in pans on wire racks 10 minutes. Remove from pans to wire racks, and cool completely (about 45 minutes).

4. Spread Fluffy White Frosting between layers; top each layer with ½ cup coconut. Spread remaining frosting on top and sides of cake; sprinkle with remaining coconut.

FLUFFY WHITE FROSTING

makes: about 5 cups   hands-on time: 15 min.
total time: 55 min.

1¾	cups sugar	½	tsp. cream of tartar
3	egg whites	1	tsp. vanilla extract

1. Cook sugar and ½ cup water in a heavy saucepan over medium heat, stirring constantly, until mixture is clear. Cook, without stirring, to soft ball stage (240°).

2. Beat egg whites and cream of tartar at medium-high speed with an electric mixer until soft peaks form. Continue beating egg whites while slowly adding hot sugar syrup. Beat at high speed 5 to 6 minutes or until frosting is thick enough to spread, using a spatula to guide the egg whites toward the beaters and scraping sides of bowl as necessary. Add vanilla, and beat until smooth.

Easton says that nobody can make coconut cake like his grandmother. This is her from-scratch recipe, which features a fluffy white frosting.

Fresh coconut is key. Use a vegetable peeler to make large shreds or curls of fresh coconut; use a box grater for smaller shreds. If you prefer bagged coconut, choose an unsweetened one with moist, relatively small shreds.

❝THESE RIBS ARE TENDER LIKE THEY OUGHT TO BE, AND THE SAUCE TENDS TOWARD THE SWEET SIDE. IF YOU PREFER MORE KICK, ADD A BIT MORE HOT SAUCE. SERVE WITH WHITE BREAD, COLESLAW, AND A WET NAPKIN.❞

BABY BACK RIBS

makes: 4 (3-rib) servings   **hands-on time: 20 min.**
total time: 2 hours

<table>
<tr><td>1</td><td>slab baby back pork ribs (about 2½ to 3 lb.)</td><td>¼</td><td>cup honey</td></tr>
<tr><td></td><td>Table salt</td><td>½</td><td>tsp. dry mustard</td></tr>
<tr><td></td><td>Salt-free garlic-and-herb seasoning blend</td><td></td><td>Several dashes hot sauce</td></tr>
<tr><td>1</td><td>cup brown sugar-flavored barbecue sauce</td><td>1</td><td>tsp. steak sauce</td></tr>
</table>

1. Rinse and pat ribs dry. If desired, remove thin membrane from the back of ribs by slicing into it with a knife and then pulling it off. (This will make ribs more tender.) Lightly sprinkle ribs with salt and garlic-and-herb seasoning; set aside.

2. Whisk together barbecue sauce and next 4 ingredients in a small bowl; set aside.

3. Light one side of grill, heating to 300° to 350° (medium); leave other side unlit.* Place ribs on oiled grill rack over unlit side, and cover the grill. Grill ribs 1 hour, turning every 15 to 20 minutes. Baste ribs with barbecue sauce mixture, and continue grilling over low heat 30 minutes or until glazed and tender, turning once.

4. Remove ribs from grill, and let rest 10 minutes. Cut ribs, slicing between bones. Serve with remaining sauce.

*For an easy oven version, bake the ribs at 325°, proceeding as directed for grilling.

NOTE: We tested with Mrs. Dash Garlic & Herb Seasoning Blend and A.1. Steak Sauce.

★ ★ ★

Easton's stepmother, Debbie Corbin, is quick to fix this dish, one of his favorites, one of his favorites, whenever he's home—and especially on his birthday. Whether you do the ribs on the grill or in the oven, they are a fun, sticky mess to eat.

★ ★ ★

Sarah Darling

This farm girl from a small Iowa community moved to Nashville more than a decade ago. As her career continues to rise and she's touring more and more, Sarah's found that baking is one of the best ways to relax.

Sarah Darling's always got something baking in the oven—pecan pie, apple crisp, sweet and savory tarts, or her latest obsession, French macarons. "To me, baking is therapeutic," Sarah notes.

Baking comes naturally to this singer-songwriter, whose mother and grandmother both loved to cook and bake. Clearly, she has inherited that passion.

Sarah grew up on a farm in Mitchellville, Iowa, a small agrarian community about 30 minutes east of Des Moines. Her extended family all lived within a few miles of each other. "The thing I remember the most is our dinner after church on Sundays," she says. Her Uncle Steve brought killer baked beans. Her mother made what she called "broccoli sunshine salad" that featured lots of bacon. "It was amazing. People were upset if it wasn't on the table."

Sarah was the dessert person—she remembers making lots of fudge pies. In the fall, the family could count on Grandma Alice to offer up her pumpkin bars topped with a generous spread of cream cheese icing. "There's really nothing better than one of her bars with a cup of coffee," says Sarah.

An only child, Sarah spent summers with her grandparents. And if she wasn't cooking in the kitchen with her grandmother, she was likely with her grandfather listening to country music. "He loved Johnny Cash and Patsy Cline," she says. "He is also just an amazing person and one of the most influential people in my life." During the time she spent with her grandfather, Sarah developed her love for the songs she now writes and sings. "You take the way you grew up, and it shines through your music," she explains.

albums

Sarah's debut album, *Every Monday Morning*, was released in 2009.

Since her Grand Ole Opry debut in February 2011, Sarah Darling has performed there more than 35 times.

"I'm a big believer that small towns are where big dreams are born," Sarah adds, and after she graduated from high school about 11 years ago, she moved straight to Nashville. For years, she played any stage that would let her and made ends meet working as a waitress in a steak house. She caught her break in 2008 and released her debut album, *Every Monday Morning,* the next year. In 2011, Sarah performed for the first time at the Grand Ole Opry, and since then she has returned to play there more than 35 times.

Even with her current hectic tour schedule, Sarah still loves to cook when she's home. And her repertoire is beginning to broaden into a more international realm. She thanks her husband, James Muriel, for that. He is a graphic designer who grew up in London, and the two of them kept up a very long distance relationship for about a year before they were married last April.

She says that "Skype cooking" (using a webcam and the Internet) helped make that a lot easier. "We would be cooking the same thing at the same time," she explains, giggling. "It was sweet, but the time difference was just crazy! It would be really late for him and really early for me."

Of course, these days they now cook together. She's fallen for his banoffee pie, a traditional British dessert made with bananas, cream, and toffee. "He's an incredible cook," she says. "But he's more 'follow-the-recipe,' and I'm more experimental."

That's true even when she's baking—occasionally, she'll stray from the recipe. "I can admit that my pecan pie is amazing," she says. "And it's because I add more butter and vanilla to the recipe. I don't like to subtract things—I add."

"THERE'S REALLY NOTHING BETTER THAN ONE OF MY GRANDMOTHER'S PUMPKIN BARS WITH A CUP OF COFFEE."

GRANDMA ALICE'S PUMPKIN BARS

makes: 3 dozen   hands-on time: 30 min.
total time: 1 hour, 35 min., including frosting

4 eggs, lightly beaten	1 tsp. baking soda
2 cups sugar	Pinch of table salt
1 cup vegetable oil	1 (16-oz.) can pumpkin
2 cups all-purpose flour	1 cup chopped walnuts or
2 tsp. baking powder	pecans (optional)
2 tsp. ground cinnamon	Cream Cheese Frosting
1½ tsp. pumpkin pie spice	

1. Preheat oven to 350°. Line a 12- x 18-inch baking pan with aluminum foil. Grease foil lightly; set aside.

2. Whisk together eggs, sugar, and oil in a large bowl; set aside.

3. Whisk together flour and next 5 ingredients in a medium bowl. Add flour mixture to egg mixture, stirring well. Stir pumpkin into batter. Fold in nuts, if desired. Pour batter into prepared baking pan.

4. Bake at 350° for 20 to 25 minutes or until toothpick inserted in center comes out clean. Cool in pan on wire rack 15 minutes. Lift bars from pan by grasping edges of foil, and transfer to a wire rack. Cool completely.

5. Spread Cream Cheese Frosting over top, and cut into 36 (1½- x 3-inch) bars.

CREAM CHEESE FROSTING

3 oz. cream cheese, softened	2 cups powdered sugar
6 Tbsp. butter or margarine, softened	2 tsp. vanilla extract
	1 tsp. milk

1. Combine cream cheese and butter, and beat at medium speed with an electric mixer until creamy. Reduce mixer speed to low; gradually add powdered sugar, beating until light and fluffy. Add vanilla extract and milk, and beat until spreading consistency.

★ ★ ★

Moist and mild, these easy bars are perfect for a crowd. One big pan makes 3 dozen oblong bars, and you can cut 'em smaller if the whole neighborhood's invited.

★ ★ ★

"PEOPLE ALWAYS LAUGH WHEN I SAY 'GORILLA BREAD.' IT'S STUFFED DOUGH—COME ON, YOU CAN'T GO WRONG WITH THAT!"

GORILLA BREAD

makes: 12 servings   hands-on time: 30 min.
total time: 1 hour, 5 min.

★ ★ ★

Sarah, who is big on breakfast and brunch, says that if the candied nut coating of her Gorilla Bread doesn't win your heart, the gooey pocket of cream cheese inside each piece surely will.

★ ★ ★

½ cup sugar
3 tsp. ground cinnamon
½ cup butter
1 cup firmly packed brown sugar
1 (8-oz.) pkg. cream cheese
2 (12-oz.) cans refrigerated biscuits
1½ cups chopped walnuts

1. Preheat oven to 375°. Stir together sugar and cinnamon in a small bowl; set aside.

2. Melt butter in a small saucepan over low heat. Add brown sugar, and cook, stirring constantly, 4 to 5 minutes or until sugar dissolves and mixture is smooth; set aside.

3. Cut cream cheese evenly into 20 cubes. Flatten biscuits into ¼-inch-thick rounds. Sprinkle each biscuit with ½ tsp. cinnamon-sugar mixture. Place a cream cheese cube in center of each biscuit. Wrap and seal biscuit dough around cream cheese.

4. Sprinkle ½ cup walnuts in the bottom of a lightly greased 14-cup Bundt pan. Arrange half of the prepared biscuits over nuts. Sprinkle with half of remaining cinnamon-sugar mixture. Spoon half of melted butter mixture over biscuits, and sprinkle with ½ cup walnuts. Repeat layers with remaining biscuits, cinnamon-sugar mixture, melted butter mixture, and walnuts.

5. Bake at 375° for 30 minutes or until bubbly and golden. Remove from oven to a wire rack; cool 5 minutes. Invert onto a serving plate, and serve immediately.

NOTE: We tested with Pillsbury Simply Buttermilk Biscuits.

SARAH DARLING

Alecia Davis

Alecia Davis began modeling when she was a teenager, a path that eventually led to dishing with country's biggest celebrities as a host on CMT. When she's home, she entertains, sharing recipes she learned from and, in some cases, makes better than her mother.

Alecia Davis has always enjoyed cooking. When she was young, she liked to watch her mother in the kitchen, and she devoured cookbooks like novels, curling up with them during Christmas and other school vacations to divine the art of cooking. But because this CMT show host (you've seen her on *Hot 20 Countdown* and *#1 Music and a Movie*) splits her time between Los Angeles and Nashville, she rarely gets the chance to slow down and really prepare a meal.

Alecia's life has moved pretty quickly since she won a national modeling competition at the age of 15. She began traveling overseas—Italy, France, Spain, and Germany—to pose for international magazine photo shoots and walk fashion show runways. Her modeling career eventually brought her close to home. Alecia grew up outside of Nashville, in Brentwood, Tennessee, which made for a comfortable fit when she was cast in country music videos for Vince Gill, Garth Brooks, Toby Keith, and other stars. (If you stumble upon the album cover of *Music for All Occasions* by The Mavericks, you'll see Alecia playfully perched beneath a red umbrella.)

The work was good, but Alecia wasn't quite content to merely strike a pose. She was naturally curious, so she took a break from modeling and studied broadcast journalism at both Middle Tennessee State University in Murfreesboro, Tennessee, and Lipscomb University in Nashville. This opened the door to television, and Alecia was soon reporting live from the red carpet and sitting down for interviews with some of the most well-known personalities in the entertainment world.

"I never intended to become a model/actress or host, but I'm so blessed and grateful to have those opportunities," she has said. "I've interviewed some incredible people, a few who've become dear friends; traveled to amazing places; and experienced a journey that otherwise I would have never known."

Alecia, who works as a television host for CMT, is best known for cohosting *Hot 20 Countdown* and *#1 Music and a Movie.*

On those special occasions when her journey brings her back home, she makes cooking a social event for her and her friends. And it's a safe bet that her mother's Hello Dollies will make an appearance for dessert. "They are a staple, and everyone loves them," says Alecia. "People don't necessarily know what's in them, but they keep coming back." The rich bars are an unbeatable combination of chocolate, coconut, pecans, and sweetened condensed milk over a graham cracker crust. Alecia says she has made them so many times that she now makes them better than her mother. "She'll tell you that, too," remarks Alecia, who believes her mother doesn't use enough condensed milk. "It just makes them creamier."

Healthy competition aside, Alecia's mother has had a huge influence on her life. She remembers that when she was 11 or 12, many were struggling financially in a down economy. Her family would join other families for dinner, and her mother would make what Alecia now calls My Favorite Lasagna. "Dishes like these could feed a lot of people," she says. "It was everyone coming together."

Today, Alecia's family still has a lot of mouths to feed, especially during the holidays. She has four older brothers ("You can imagine I was fighting to get food growing up," she says with a laugh) and 15 nieces and nephews. With that many different palates in the family, sometimes it's a challenge to find food everyone likes. Her mother's Mandarin Almond Salad—crunchy and sweet, with just the right amount of rice vinegar to keep it balanced—is never an issue, though. It has always been a part of their Thanksgiving dinner. "It's the one salad we'll all eat," Alecia says.

MANDARIN-ALMOND SALAD

makes: 8 servings   **hands-on time: 35 min.**   **total time: 45 min.**

* * *

Crunchy and sweet Mandarin Almond Salad was a Thanksgiving staple at the Davis house, mainly because it was the one dish that Alecia and her four older brothers all liked.

* * *

Parchment paper
4   Tbsp. sugar, divided
½   cup slivered almonds
¼   cup vegetable oil
2   Tbsp. rice vinegar
1   Tbsp. finely chopped fresh parsley
½   tsp. table salt
⅛   tsp. hot pepper sauce
1   bunch red leaf lettuce
1   (11-oz.) can mandarin oranges, drained
1   small red onion, sliced

1. Line a baking sheet with parchment paper. In a small skillet, melt 3 Tbsp. sugar over medium-low heat. Add almonds, and stir until coated. Pour almonds onto prepared baking sheet, and place on a wire rack; cool completely, break into small pieces, and set aside.

2. Combine oil, next 4 ingredients, and remaining sugar in a jar with a tight-fitting lid; shake well.

3. Combine lettuce, oranges, onion, and almonds in large salad bowl. Shake dressing well, pour over salad, and toss to coat.

TIP

If you can find fresh mandarin oranges, substitute them for the canned version to add even more flavor to this delicious salad.

ALECIA DAVIS

❝MY MOTHER DID A LOT OF COOKING, AND AS MUCH AS SHE COULD, SHE ALWAYS MADE SURE WE WERE AROUND THE DINNER TABLE AT NIGHT.❞

MY FAVORITE LASAGNA

**makes: 8 servings   hands-on time: 20 min.
total time: 1 hour, 20 min.**

2	lb. ground beef
1	(24-oz.) jar pasta sauce
1	(14-oz.) jar pizza sauce
1	(8-oz.) container sour cream
1	(8-oz.) package cream cheese, softened
½	medium-size green bell pepper, chopped
1	(4-oz.) can chopped green chiles, drained

1	(4-oz.) can mushroom pieces and stems, drained
1	bunch green onions, chopped
8	dried precooked lasagna noodles
1	(8-oz.) pkg. shredded Cheddar cheese
1	(8-oz.) pkg. shredded part-skim mozzarella cheese

Garnish: sliced green onions

1. Preheat oven to 350°. Brown beef in a large skillet 6 to 8 minutes or until meat crumbles and is no longer pink; drain. Stir sauces into meat.

2. Stir together sour cream and next 5 ingredients in a medium bowl.

3. Spoon 1 cup meat mixture into a lightly greased 13- x 9-inch baking dish. Arrange 4 noodles over sauce, top with 1½ cups meat mixture, one-half of sour cream mixture, one-third of Cheddar cheese, and one-third of mozzarella cheese. Repeat layers, and top with remaining 1½ cups meat mixture; cover tightly with aluminum foil.

4. Bake at 350° for 45 minutes. Uncover and sprinkle evenly with remaining Cheddar and mozzarella cheeses. Bake 10 more minutes. Let stand 5 minutes before serving.

★ ★ ★

Alecia remembers her mother making this lasagna and sharing it at community dinners held during tough financial times. "Dishes like these could feed a lot of people. It was everyone coming together."

★ ★ ★

NO MATTER WHERE SHE IS—LOS ANGELES OR NASHVILLE—ALECIA'S FRIENDS DEVOUR THESE EASY-TO-MAKE, ULTRA-DECADENT BARS. ❝THEY DON'T NECESSARILY KNOW WHAT'S IN THEM, BUT THEY KEEP COMING BACK.❞

HELLO DOLLIES

makes: 24 servings   **hands-on time: 20 min.**
total time: 1 hour, 30 min.

★ ★ ★

Cut these bars small, and pass 'em around to share the calories—and the love.

★ ★ ★

½   cup unsalted butter
1   cup graham cracker crumbs
1   cup sweetened shredded coconut
1   cup toasted pecan halves

1   cup semisweet chocolate morsels
1   (14-oz.) can sweetened condensed milk

1. Preheat oven to 350°. Place aluminum foil in an 8-inch square aluminum baking pan, allowing foil to extend over edges of pan. Melt butter in prepared pan.

2. Layer graham cracker crumbs and next 3 ingredients over butter. Pour condensed milk evenly over chocolate morsels.

3. Bake at 350° for 30 minutes or until top is golden and edges are bubbly. Remove pan to a wire rack, and cool 15 minutes. Use foil to lift out of pan, and place on wire rack; cool completely (about 30 minutes). Peel off foil, and cut into 1½- x 2-inch rectangles.

☞ TIP ☜

If for some reason you have leftovers, store them in an airtight container with wax paper between the layers.

Allison DeMarcus

This CMT host, former beauty queen, and wife of a country music star loves casseroles. But that's not just because they are Southern staples—she believes they represent the importance of community and the strength found in neighborly relationships.

Allison DeMarcus tells a pretty good meet-the-parents story. She and her then boyfriend, Jay, had only been seeing each other a few months when she brought him home to Jackson, Tennessee, to meet her mother and father. Jay—the bassist, pianist, and vocalist for the country group Rascal Flatts—was nervous about meeting her dad, whom Allison describes as a stoic Vietnam veteran. "My dad used to tell me he always wanted boys to be intimidated by him," she says with a laugh. Jay initially fell into that category, but he soon relaxed when he saw the menu for the evening. Allison's mother had decided to serve tetrazzini, one of her specialties. And in case that pasta dish wasn't enough, she also made a pan of homemade macaroni and cheese—Allison had given her mother the hot tip that mac and cheese was Jay's favorite. From then on, Jay felt right at home, and their courtship blossomed.

Allison has great love for her hometown of Jackson because her family's roots are there. Her family is a tightly knit bunch, and she grew up with both sets of grandparents nearby. "My parents knew I was about to mess up before I did!" she recalls. Once she began to compete seriously in beauty pageants, she traveled and met lots of different types of people.

She turned out to be excellent at competing and went on to represent the state of Tennessee in the Miss Teen USA, Miss USA, and Miss America pageants. Those experiences led to a modeling career, and for one gig, she was cast in a video for the Rascal Flatts song "These Days." (Did you see that coming?) That, of course, is when she met Jay.

Allison's pageant work served her well. She

developed poise and was comfortable around famous people. This, as well as a healthy curiosity, translated perfectly on camera when she landed a role as a red carpet award show correspondent for CMT. In addition to appearing on numerous shows on the network, she's currently hosting CMT's new cooking show, *Reel Eats.*

In Allison's family, cooking and sharing good food has always been an important way to bond. When she was growing up, her grandparents alternated hosting big family meals. Her grandmothers still live in Jackson, and one of them, who is in her nineties, continues to cook favorite dishes for spreads at family functions—such as her slow-cooked macaroni and cheese (yes, more mac and cheese!) that must be stirred for an hour.

Allison and Jay's children Madeline and Dylan are young—one is 3 years old and the other is 13 months—so cooking and sharing meals is a big part of family life. When Jay is home, all four spend time in the kitchen. "Jay is actually the real chef in the family," says Allison. "When he comes off the road, he finds cooking is a great way to unwind." She especially loves his lasagna and chili. "He does all the heavy cooking, while I take care of the kids and keep them wrangled."

Allison doesn't do a lot of experimental cooking. She likes to stay in her comfort zone and brags just a tad by admitting that she makes a mean casserole. "You just have to know how to make one if you're from the South," she says matter-of-factly.

In an interesting way, that love of casseroles speaks to her strong desire for community. She recalls that when she and Jay were first married,

Allison DeMarcus works as a host and correspondent for CMT, including the red carpet show at the CMT Music Awards and CMT's *Hot 20 Countdown.* She's now the host of the network's new cooking show, *Reel Eats.*

(continued on page 84)

they lived outside Nashville in a house on a beautiful property. It was nice and peaceful, but the problem for her was that there weren't many people living nearby. "I told him I had to raise my children in a neighborhood." So they moved back into Nashville, where she could easily make and share her casseroles with neighbors and family members.

It's no surprise, then, to learn about Allison's Christmas Day brunch family tradition—serving her mother's Breakfast Casserole, which features lots of sausage and Cheddar cheese.

Another go-to has become John Murphy's Corn Casserole; John is the wardrobe stylist for Rascal Flatts and a good friend. He also happens to be a fine cook who always shares recipes. "John's corn casserole has all the good things in it," notes Allison, "and it makes me look like a much better cook than I am."

Allison and Jay's young daughter and son really love Jay's mother's recipe Miss Caron's Pizza Casserole, which is loaded with ground beef, pepperoni, and elbow macaroni. "Jay's part Italian, and he grew up on the dish," Allison notes.

"JAY IS ACTUALLY THE REAL CHEF IN THE FAMILY," SAYS ALLISON. SHE ESPECIALLY LOVES HIS LASAGNA AND CHILI. **"HE DOES ALL THE HEAVY COOKING, WHILE I TAKE CARE OF THE KIDS AND KEEP THEM WRANGLED."**

ALLISON ON CASSEROLES: "THAT'S A SOUTHERN THING. YOU JUST HAVE TO KNOW HOW TO MAKE ONE IF YOU'RE FROM THE SOUTH."

BREAKFAST CASSEROLE

makes: 8 servings   hands-on time: 30 min.
total time: 1 hour, 50 min., plus 8 hours for chilling

The casserole is Allison's mother's recipe, and became an instant DeMarcus family Christmas breakfast tradition.

- 6 slices white bread, crusts removed and cubed
- 1 (1-lb.) package mild ground pork sausage, cooked and drained
- 8 large eggs, lightly beaten
- 2 cups milk
- 1½ cups (6 oz.) shredded mild Cheddar cheese
- 1 tsp. dry mustard
- 1 tsp. table salt
- ½ tsp. freshly ground black pepper

1. Place cubed bread in a lightly greased 13- x 9-inch baking dish. Crumble sausage over bread.

2. Combine eggs and next 5 ingredients in a large bowl, and pour over sausage. Cover and chill at least 8 hours.

3. Remove baking dish from refrigerator 30 minutes before baking. Preheat oven to 375°.

4. Bake at 375° for 40 to 45 minutes. Let stand 10 minutes before serving.

NOTE: We tested with Jimmy Dean Regular Premium Pork Sausage.

TIP

Don't forget to prepare this the night before you plan to serve it, and make sure to seal it with a layer of plastic wrap before you put it in the refrigerator to chill.

ALLISON DEMARCUS

❝ JOHN MURPHY IS A FRIEND OF MINE WHO WORKS FOR RASCAL FLATTS. THIS IS HIS MAMA'S RECIPE FOR CORN CASSEROLE, AND IT'S DIVINE.❞

JOHN MURPHY'S CORN CASSEROLE

**makes: 6 to 8 servings   hands-on time: 15 min.
total time: 1 hour, 15 min.**

2	(14 ¾-oz.) cans cream-style corn	1	sleeve of saltine crackers, crushed (36 crackers)
1	cup milk		Sea salt
2	large eggs, lightly beaten		Freshly ground black pepper
½	yellow onion, chopped		
½	medium-size green bell pepper, chopped		

1. Preheat oven to 350°. Combine corn and next 5 ingredients in a large bowl. Add salt and pepper to taste. Pour into a lightly greased 11- x 7-inch baking dish. Bake at 350° for 1 hour or until lightly browned and set.

★ ★ ★

This easy casserole is comfort food at its best: quick, wholesome, and delicious.

★ ★ ★

THE KIDS LOVE JAY'S MOTHER'S PIZZA CASSEROLE. "JAY'S PART ITALIAN, AND HE GREW UP ON THIS DISH."

MISS CARON'S PIZZA CASSEROLE

**makes: 8 servings   hands-on time: 20 min.
total time: 1 hour, 5 min.**

This delicious make-ahead dish is loaded with ground beef and pepperoni. Top it with fresh oregano for even more healthy flavor.

1   lb. ground beef
½   yellow onion, chopped
8   oz. uncooked elbow macaroni
2   (14-oz.) jars pizza sauce
1   (3.5-oz.) package pepperoni slices
1   (8-oz.) package shredded part-skim mozzarella cheese
Garnish: fresh oregano leaves

1. Preheat oven to 350°. Brown meat with onion in a large skillet over medium heat 7 to 8 minutes; drain and set aside.

2. Prepare macaroni according to package directions. Stir pizza sauce and cooked macaroni into meat mixture.

3. Spoon half of meat mixture into a lightly greased 13- x 9-inch baking dish. Top with half of pepperoni and half of shredded cheese; repeat layers.

4. Bake at 350° for 25 to 30 minutes or until bubbly.

ALLISON DEMARCUS

Brett Eldredge

This singer-songwriter grew up fishing on a lake in a small Illinois town. When he's not on the road these days—a rare occurrence—he sneaks off to cast a line.

Brett Eldredge has wanted to sing for as long as he can remember. "Truthfully, I always had the dream," he says. "I always knew I would be a singer. I didn't know what you had to do to get there, but I knew I would do it."

He started by performing wherever he could—golf courses, backyard parties, corner cafes, county fairs, and talent shows in and around his hometown of Paris, Illinois, a small agricultural community bordered by cornfields and cow pastures that are tilled with hard work and tended with humility, and filled with legions of fans. "I'm reminded every day just how important being from that town is," he says. "People supported me, and the pride I have from being from there is still such a part of me."

Brett grew up on a lake, and at every free moment, he'd steal away to fish. In the dead of winter, he'd cut holes in the ice to drop a line. In the summer heat, he'd try to catch catfish at night. "When you're out there on the water and there's no ambient light, all you see is the moon and stars lighting up the lake," he says. "There's a wonderful quietness on the water."

Having a house on the water meant his friends were always visiting, and they spent summer days on the family deck boat (nicknamed "Bessie"). To keep the boys fed, Brett's mother, Robin Eldredge, whipped up large servings of her Sweet and Sour Salsa, which features mango, white vinegar, and

albums

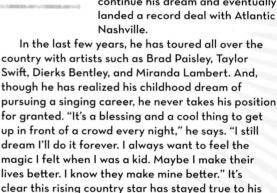

Brett Eldredge's first album, *Bring You Back,* was released in 2013.

brown sugar. "It's refreshing and the perfect mix of sweet and savory," Brett notes. "It goes with anything in the summertime." They also loved her baked goods, especially Golda's Brownies, a chocolate chip-laced treat inherited from Brett's great-grandmother Golda Hilpert.

As a boy, Brett was a big country music fan. He says he memorized every song he heard by country duo Kix Brooks and Ronnie Dunn. But he was also drawn to soulful crooners, like Ray Charles and Frank Sinatra, whose styles seeped into his own. You can hear that influence in his powerful, slightly gravelly voice. He sang every chance he had while he was attending Elmhurst College, a small liberal arts school west of Chicago. From there, he moved to Nashville to continue his dream and eventually landed a record deal with Atlantic Nashville.

In the last few years, he has toured all over the country with artists such as Brad Paisley, Taylor Swift, Dierks Bentley, and Miranda Lambert. And, though he has realized his childhood dream of pursuing a singing career, he never takes his position for granted. "It's a blessing and a cool thing to get up in front of a crowd every night," he says. "I still dream I'll do it forever. I always want to feel the magic I felt when I was a kid. Maybe I make their lives better. I know they make mine better." It's clear this rising country star has stayed true to his humble roots.

BRETT ELDREDGE'S MOTHER MADE THIS RECIPE OFTEN WHEN BRETT'S FRIENDS CAME TO VISIT. "IT'S REFRESHING AND THE PERFECT MIX OF SWEET AND SAVORY."

SWEET-AND-SOUR SALSA

**makes: about 3 cups   hands-on time: 20 min.
total time: 1 hour, 20 min.**

This salsa is very adaptable, keeps well in the refrigerator, and is great as a topping for fish. You may add tomatoes or additional garden veggies, if you like.

1	large mango or 2 large peaches, peeled and cubed
1½	cups diced bell pepper (a mixture of red, yellow, orange, and green)
¼	cup chopped red onion
2	Tbsp. olive oil
2	Tbsp. brown sugar or honey
1	Tbsp. red or white wine vinegar or apple cider vinegar
	Table salt
	Freshly ground black pepper
3	Tbsp. chopped fresh cilantro

1. Combine mango, bell pepper, and onion in a medium bowl.

2. Whisk together olive oil and next 2 ingredients in a small bowl. Add salt and pepper to taste, and drizzle over mango mixture. Toss to coat. Cover and chill 1 hour or until ready to serve. Stir in cilantro just before serving.

TIP

Don't judge the ripeness of a mango by its color. Instead, squeeze the fruit gently. if it gives slightly, then it's ready to eat.

BRETT'S MOTHER ALSO BAKED HIS FAVORITE BROWNIES USING THE OLD FAMILY RECIPE FROM BRETT'S GREAT-GRANDMOTHER GOLDA HILPERT.

GOLDA'S BROWNIES

makes: 20 servings   hands-on time: 20 min.
total time: 1 hour, 55 min.

4   (1-oz.) squares unsweetened chocolate baking squares*
²⁄₃   cup butter or margarine
2   cups sugar
4   large eggs
½   cup flour
1   tsp. baking soda
1   tsp. table salt
1   cup semisweet chocolate chips
½   cup chopped pecans (optional)
Vanilla ice cream (optional)
Chocolate syrup (optional)

1. Preheat oven to 350°. Line bottom and sides of a 13- x 9-inch baking pan with aluminum foil, allowing 2 to 3 inches to extend over sides; lightly grease foil.

2. Microwave chocolate squares and butter in a large microwave-safe bowl on 'high' setting 1½ to 2 minutes or until melted and smooth, stirring at 30-second intervals. Whisk in sugar. Add eggs, 1 at a time, whisking just until blended after each addition. Whisk in flour, baking soda, and salt.

3. Pour mixture into prepared pan. Sprinkle chocolate chips and pecans, if desired, over mixture.

4. Bake at 350° for 30 to 35 minutes or until a wooden pick inserted in center comes out with a few moist crumbs. Cool completely on a wire rack (about 1 hour). Lift brownies from pan, using foil sides as handles. Gently remove foil, and cut brownies into 20 squares. Serve with ice cream and chocolate syrup, if desired.

* You may substitute ³⁄₄ cup unsweetened cocoa combined with ¼ cup vegetable oil for the 4 (1-oz.) squares unsweetened chocolate baking squares.

★ ★ ★

Chocolate baking squares and chocolate chips give Golda's Brownies extra oomph.

★ ★ ★

GUARDIAN ANGEL ★ SMALL TOWN KID ★ I CALL THE U.S.A.
HERE'S TO YOU ✒ LONELY ALL THE TIME ♫ When it Rain
ALWAYS THE LOVE SONGS ♫ Radio Waves ♫ ENOUGH IS ENOUGH
Throw And Go ★ GUINEVERE ★ Get In the Car

and Drive ★ ★ ★ JET BLACK AND JEALOUS ♫
Mystery in the Making ★ HOW SHOULD I KNOW ★ Home
EVEN IF IT BREAKS YOUR HEART ♫ CRAZY GIRL
EVERY OTHER MEMORY ✒ On My Way ♫ SKELETONS ★ ★ ★

Eli Young Band

From Texas college kids jamming in a garage and scouring sofas for fast-food money to men with families and a country music act touring nationally, the members of the Eli Young Band have come a long way. Of course, they remain young at heart.

First things first: Eli Young is not a dude in the band. The name comes from lead singer Mike Eli and guitarist James Young, who met in the late 1990s at the University of North Texas in Denton. With drummer Chris Thompson and bass player Jon Jones, they found their sound—a high-energy blend of country and rock—while they were jamming in a garage. They'd haul their gear to gigs in a couple of pickup trucks. When it came to food, "We pretty much ate anything we could get at McDonald's with the change we found in our couch," Chris says with a laugh.

The boys moved on in many ways, trading their pickup trucks for vans, and then a touring bus. After more than a decade together, they decided they needed to eat better. They began seeking out healthy restaurants and bringing coolers packed with homemade dishes. "Those coolers were really where we started talking about family recipes," says Chris. "We were learning about where we all came from. Everyone had his own take on salad or chicken."

Chris's take on chicken comes from his wife. Candace's Perfect Roast Chicken won his heart the first time she made it for him. "I had never seen a chicken cooked like this outside of Thanksgiving or Christmas," he recalls. "I thought, 'Is this a holiday?' No, it was just a Monday night." Candace's family tree is full of people who love cooking, grilling, and

baking. "She's well-versed in the kitchen," says Chris. "I totally lucked out." Chris says he often feels like he's a student in the kitchen when she is cooking.

When it comes to grilling, Chris says he and guitarist James Young are the pros. "It's our wheelhouse and comfort zone," says Chris. James's wife, Abby, also has a solid culinary pedigree. Many of her recipes, including Cream of Green Chile Soup, come from her grandmother Sue Sims, who is a professional chef. "This soup can be enjoyed in the hottest of summer or in the winter," says James.

Of the foursome, lead singer Mike Eli and bass player Jon Jones have the greatest passion for food. "Mike takes charge in the kitchen," notes Chris, who remembers that Mike began making his Beefy Onion Spread when they were bachelors living together in the early 2000s. "That dish had some personality."

And when they need food and wine recommendations, everyone goes to Jon, whose family is in the restaurant business. He's also the go-to source for comfort food, including the recipe for his Aunt Donna's Chicken and Noodles. "It has been passed down for many generations," says Jon. "We have a very large extended family, and this was a staple at every gathering growing up."

There's no more garage band jamming these days. "We've grown up a little bit," says Chris with a smile, "A little bit—not a lot."

❧ albums & awards ❧

The Eli Young Band includes Mike Eli, Chris Thompson, James Young, and Jon Jones.

Eli Young Band, 2002

Level, 2005

Live at the Jolly Fox, 2006

Jet Black & Jealous, 2008

Life at Best, 2011

10,000 Towns, 2013

Received the Academy of Country Music Award Song of the Year for "Crazy Girl" in 2012.

"We don't set out to write just one kind of song," says guitarist James Young.

CREAM OF GREEN CHILE SOUP

makes: 6 to 8 servings (8 cups)   hands-on time: 50 min.
total time: 1 hour, 20 min., including Apache Cakes and
Cranberry Pico

2	cups reduced-sodium fat-free chicken broth		4	(4-oz.) cans chopped green chiles
¼	cup chopped onion		2	Tbsp. fresh lime juice
2	garlic cloves, minced			Apache Cakes or tortilla chips
2	cups plain yogurt, strained			Cranberry Pico (page 102)
2	(8-oz.) packages ⅓-less-fat cream cheese			

1. Bring chicken broth, onion, and garlic to a boil in a medium saucepan over medium heat; reduce heat, and simmer 10 minutes or until onion is translucent. Remove from heat; drain onions and garlic, reserving broth.

2. Combine yogurt, next 3 ingredients, onion, and garlic in container of a blender; puree until smooth. Add 1 cup reserved broth, and blend until smooth.

3. Serve hot or cold with Apache Cakes or tortilla chips and Cranberry Pico.

APACHE CAKES

makes: 6 to 8 servings (16 cakes)   hands-on time: 20 min.
total time: 35 min.

¾	cup all-purpose flour		2	extra-large eggs, lightly beaten
1¼	cups stone-ground yellow cornmeal		1	cup frozen corn, thawed
2	Tbsp. sugar		½	cup (2 oz.) shredded extra-sharp Cheddar cheese
2	tsp. baking powder		2	jalapeño peppers, seeded and finely chopped
½	tsp. table salt			
1	cup milk			
¼	cup canola oil			

1. Combine flour and next 4 ingredients in a medium bowl.

2. Combine milk, oil, and eggs; add to dry ingredients, stirring just until moistened. Stir in remaining ingredients. If not using immediately, cover batter, and chill up to 2 days.

3. Pour about 3 Tbsp. batter for each cake onto a hot, lightly greased griddle. Cook cakes, in batches, 3 minutes or until tops are covered with bubbles and edges look cooked; turn and cook 2 more minutes.

★ ★ ★

Lead guitarist James Young says the extent of his cooking lies mostly outside on the grill. His wife, however, has been given many recipes from her grandmother, who is a professional chef. The soup can be made a day ahead (it gets better with age, the original recipe says) and may be served hot or cold.

★ ★ ★

"MY MOM ALWAYS MADE BEEFY ONION SPREAD WHENEVER WE HAD COMPANY GROWING UP," SAYS LEAD SINGER MIKE ELI. "IT'S A COMFORT FOOD FOR ME. I LOVE TO MAKE IT FOR GUESTS."

CRANBERRY PICO

makes: about 1½ cups   hands-on time: 15 min.
total time: 15 min.

8	oz. fresh or frozen cranberries (do not thaw)	1	small jalapeño pepper, seeded and chopped
⅓	cup sugar	¼	cup fresh chopped cilantro
2	green onions, chopped	1	Tbsp. lime juice

1. Pulse cranberries and sugar in bowl of food processor 3 or 4 times or until blended. Add onions and remaining ingredients; pulse until finely chopped. Cover and chill up to 5 days.

BEEFY ONION SPREAD

makes: 10 to 12 appetizer servings (3½ cups)
hands-on time: 20 min.   total time: 2 hours, 35 min.

★ ★ ★

This simple spread packs lots of flavor and is best served with whole grain crackers.

★ ★ ★

2	(8-oz.) packages cream cheese, softened	1	tsp. Worcestershire sauce
15	green onions, finely chopped		Freshly ground black pepper
1	(4.5-oz.) jar sliced dried beef, finely chopped		Whole grain wheat crackers

1. Stir together cream cheese and next 3 ingredients in a medium bowl until smooth. Cover and chill at least 2 hours.

2. Sprinkle with pepper. Serve with crackers.

NOTE: We tested with Armour Sliced Dried Beef.

"I HAD NEVER SEEN A CHICKEN LIKE THIS OUTSIDE OF THANKSGIVING OR CHRISTMAS. I THOUGHT 'IS THIS A HOLIDAY?' NO, IT WAS JUST A MONDAY NIGHT," SAYS DRUMMER CHRIS THOMPSON.

CANDACE'S PERFECT ROAST CHICKEN

**makes: 6 to 8 servings   hands-on time: 20 min.
total time: 1 hour, 35 min.**

Olive oil
1   (5- to 6-lb.) whole chicken
Kosher salt
Freshly ground black pepper
6   sprigs fresh rosemary, divided
3 to 4 garlic cloves

1   large yellow onion, cut in 2-inch pieces
1   bunch carrots with tops, trimmed and cut in 2-inch pieces
4   celery ribs, cut in 2-inch pieces

1. Preheat oven to 425°. Drizzle olive oil over chicken and inside cavities; season liberally with salt and pepper.

2. Place 2 rosemary sprigs, 1 garlic clove, and several pieces of onion, carrot, and celery in neck cavity of chicken; repeat process in lower cavity.

3. Starting at neck cavity, loosen skin, and lift skin from chicken breast with fingers. (Do not totally detach skin.) Insert remaining rosemary sprigs between skin and breasts. Carefully replace skin.

4. Tie legs together with string, if desired; tuck chicken wings under. Place chicken, breast side up, in a lightly greased shallow roasting pan. Arrange remaining vegetables and garlic around chicken. Drizzle vegetables with olive oil, and season as desired with salt and pepper.

5. Bake at 425° for 1 hour and 15 minutes or until skin is golden and crisp and a meat thermometer inserted into thigh registers 180°, turning pan occasionally for even browning. Carve and serve!

★ ★ ★

Chris says this is his favorite thing that his wife, Candace, makes. She often surprises him with it when he comes home from being on the road.

★ ★ ★

COUNTRY MUSIC'S GREATEST EATS

"THIS RECIPE HAS BEEN PASSED DOWN FOR GENERATIONS," SAYS BASS PLAYER JON JONES. "IT WAS A STAPLE AT EVERY GATHERING GROWING UP."

AUNT DONNA'S CHICKEN AND NOODLES

makes: 8 to 10 servings (12 cups)   **hands-on time: 1 hour, 15 min.**
total time: 2 hours, 40 min.

★ ★ ★

This recipe calls for a dozen egg yolks— use the egg whites to make angel food cake, a light sweet ending to this hearty meal.

★ ★ ★

2   (3-lb.) chickens
12   extra-large egg yolks
1½   tsp. table salt, plus additional salt to taste
1   cup all-purpose flour, plus more as needed

Freshly ground black pepper to taste
Hot mashed potatoes (optional)
Garnish: chopped fresh parsley

1. Bring chickens and water to cover to a boil in a large Dutch oven. Reduce heat, and simmer, partially covered, 1½ to 2 hours or until chicken is tender. Skim off foam as chicken cooks. Remove chicken; cool. Pour broth through a wire-mesh strainer into a large bowl, and discard solids. Skim off fat; return broth to Dutch oven.

2. Skin, bone, and shred chicken; cover and set aside.

3. Whisk together egg yolks and 1½ tsp. salt in a medium bowl. Add 1 cup of flour; stir until a ball of dough begins to form, adding more flour if needed.

4. Transfer dough to a floured surface; knead 8 to 10 times or until dough is smooth, adding flour as needed. (Be careful not to add too much flour, or the dough will be too stiff for rolling; a whole egg may be added if that happens.) Divide dough into four balls; let rest 5 to 10 minutes.

5. Roll 1 dough ball to ⅛-inch thickness on a floured surface to form a 12-inch round, turning dough over, and adding flour as needed to keep dough from sticking to surface or rolling pin. Set dough aside on a floured surface; sprinkle top with flour. Repeat process with remaining dough balls, stacking the rounds as you go. Cut stacked dough rounds into 12- x 3-inch strips. Stack strips on top of each other, sprinkling each layer with additional flour. Cut dough stacks crosswise into ¼-inch strips. Fluff noodles with fingers to separate. Spread noodles on a cookie sheet (noodles may be stored, covered, in the refrigerator up to 1 day).

6. Bring reserved chicken broth to a boil. Gradually stir noodles into broth; boil 5 to 8 minutes, stirring often. Add shredded chicken and salt and pepper to taste. Reduce heat; simmer over low heat, stirring occasionally, 30 minutes. Serve over mashed potatoes, if desired.

Sara Evans

Sara Evans has been singing almost as long as she can remember. This small-town farm girl from a huge family has enjoyed a wonderful career as one of country music's brightest stars.

When Sara Evans was growing up on a farm in New Franklin, Missouri, mealtimes could be a little chaotic. With seven hungry children, Sara's mother, Patricia, needed good, simple recipes that she could whip up in quantity. Taco Salad and Mama's Chili fit that order perfectly. For something sweet, she would throw together a large Missouri Dirt Cake made with vanilla pudding and Oreo chocolate sandwich cookies.

No doubt, food bonded Sara's family—but not as much as music. The Evanses had a family band, and Sara was singing in it as early as age 5. Traveling throughout Missouri, the band performed gospel and bluegrass music at church revivals and festivals. As her voice matured, Sara led the group, dreaming of Nashville and a career in country music. After a brief college stint, she discovered that she "had no other aspirations but to sing." She and one of her brothers moved to Nashville, where she waited tables at a Holiday Inn and tried to make connections.

Sara landed a record deal, and in 1997, she released her debut album *Three Chords and the Truth*. At that time, a pop sound permeated country music, but Sara wrote and recorded songs that were traditional, timeless, and reminiscent of classic country. The songs featured fiddles, mandolins, and acoustic rhythm instruments, and reflected the music of the women she had grown up emulating, including Patsy Cline, Tammy Wynette, and Patty Loveless.

In 2000, Sara released the album *Born to Fly*. The title track, which some believe to be autobiographical, tells the story of a dreamer trying to strike out on her own. "But how do you wait for Heaven?/And who has that much time?/And how do you keep your feet on the ground/When you know that you were born, you were born to fly." The song earned the County Music Association Award for Video of the Year and made Sara a superstar. Since then, she has won other awards and the chance to compete on the third season of ABC's *Dancing with the Stars*.

In 2008, she married former University of Alabama football star and sportscaster Jay Barker. The two have children from previous marriages—Sara has three and Jay has four—so once again Sara's house is home to seven kids. (Not surprisingly, they love Missouri Dirt Cake just as much as she does and often request it for their birthdays.)

After almost 20 years as a big name in country music, Sara is still touring across the country. She says she's just as young-at-heart as when she was starting out. "I feel like there's nothing that I can't do. I'm definitely more confident now than I've ever been in my life."

❧ albums & awards ❧

Sara received the Country Music Association Award for Video of the Year for "Born to Fly" in 2001.

Three Chords and the Truth, 1997

No Place That Far, 1998

Born to Fly, 2000

Restless, 2003

Real Fine Place, 2005

Stronger, 2011

Slow Me Down, 2014

In 2006, Sara received the Academy of Country Music Award for Top Female Vocalist.

WITH SEVEN HUNGRY CHILDREN, SARA'S MOM NEEDED GOOD, SIMPLE RECIPES THAT SHE COULD WHIP UP IN LARGE QUANTITIES, LIKE TACO SALAD.

Taco salad tastes best when the ingredients are combined just before serving. Sara's secret is to use nacho cheese-flavored tortilla chips.

TACO SALAD

makes: 6 servings   hands-on time: 30 min.   total time: 30 min.

1   (8-oz.) carton sour cream
1   (16-oz.) bottle creamy Italian salad dressing
1   (11-oz.) bag nacho cheese-flavored tortilla chips, crushed and divided
1   head iceberg lettuce, shredded or 1 (8-oz.) bag shredded lettuce
1   small red onion, finely chopped
2   cups cherry or grape tomatoes, halved
1   (8-oz.) package shredded Cheddar cheese
1   (16-oz.) can dark kidney beans, drained and rinsed

1. Whisk together sour cream and salad dressing in a small bowl.

2. Set aside 1 cup crushed tortilla chips. Place remaining chips in a large salad bowl. Add lettuce and next 4 ingredients. Drizzle with half of salad dressing mixture; toss.

3. Top salad with reserved crushed chips. Serve immediately with remaining dressing.

NOTE: We tested with Doritos Nacho Cheese flavored tortilla chips.

MAMA'S CHILI

makes: 6 servings **hands-on time: 20 min.**
total time: 1 hour, 15 min.

- 1 lb. ground beef
- 1 medium-size yellow onion, chopped
- 1 (1.25-oz.) packet taco seasoning
- ¼ cup brown sugar
- 1 (28-oz.) can crushed tomatoes
- 1 (16-oz.) can tomato sauce
- 1 (10¾-oz.) can tomato soup
- 1 (16-oz.) can chili beans
- 1 (16-oz.) can pork and beans

Toppings: shredded Cheddar cheese, chopped green onions

1. Cook ground beef and onion in a Dutch oven over medium heat, stirring until meat crumbles and is no longer pink. Drain; return beef mixture to Dutch oven.

2. Add taco seasoning to meat mixture; cook over medium heat, stirring constantly, 2 minutes. Stir in brown sugar and next 3 ingredients, and bring to a boil. Reduce heat to medium-low, and simmer, stirring occasionally, 30 minutes.

3. Add beans and simmer, stirring occasionally, 15 minutes or until thoroughly heated. Serve with desired toppings.

NOTE: We tested with McCormick's Original Taco Seasoning Mix and Bush's Chili Beans.

★ ★ ★

Nothing beats a hot bowlful of Mama's Chili on a cold, wet day. When Sara comes home from being on tour, this is what she wants most—and it's easy to make!

★ ★ ★

☞ TIP ☜

This is a dish that only improves with age. Double the recipe and freeze some for comfort food in a pinch.

❝THIS IS ANOTHER AMAZING DESSERT MY MOM ALWAYS MADE. SOMETIMES MY KIDS WANT IT FOR THEIR BIRTHDAY CAKE!❞

This easy peasy treat comes together quickly once the frozen whipped topping has thawed. It's waiting during the chilling time that may test your patience!

MISSOURI DIRT CAKE

makes: 12 servings   hands-on time: 20 min.
total time: 11 hours, 20 min., including thawing and chilling

- 1 (8-oz.) package cream cheese, softened
- 1 (8-oz.) carton frozen whipped topping, thawed
- 1 (5.1-oz.) box instant vanilla pudding
- 2 cups milk
- ⅓ cup powdered sugar
- 1 (14.3-oz.) package chocolate sandwich cookies (36 cookies), crushed and divided

1. Whisk together cream cheese and whipped topping in a large bowl.

2. Prepare pudding using 2 cups of milk. Fold pudding and powdered sugar into cream cheese mixture.

3. Press 3 cups of crushed cookies in a lightly greased 13- x 9-inch baking dish; set aside remaining cookies.

4. Spoon pudding mixture over cookies. Sprinkle reserved cookies over pudding. Cover and chill 3 hours. Enjoy!

NOTE: We tested with Cool Whip Original Whipped Topping and Oreo Chocolate Sandwich Cookies.

Florida Georgia Line

Brian Kelley (the Floridian) and Tyler Hubbard (straight out of Georgia) met in college and instantly clicked musically. Now, the young men's popularity comes courtesy of their original rocking, high-energy sound.

When Tyler Hubbard and Brian Kelley—the successful country duo known as Florida Georgia Line—needed some grilling pointers, their famous songwriter friend Craig Wiseman was at the ready with straightforward advice. "I told them, 'Never undercook the chicken, and never mash a burger on the grill,' " Craig remembers.

It was the summer of 2012, and Florida Georgia Line had been invited to perform on the Country Throwdown Tour. Part of their duties included commanding the grill after the shows at stops along the way. It was like a private cookout for the crew and performers, and that summer Tyler and Brian learned a lot about grilling.

Craig already knew a little something about cooking. He grew up in Hattiesburg, Mississippi, which was close enough to New Orleans and the Gulf Coast for him to be influenced by lots of Cajun foods and seafood dishes. While in Austin, Texas, one year for the South by Southwest Festival, Craig tried a Serrano Pepper Burger and decided to develop that recipe on his own. "It's a great way to take a regular burger to a whole new level," he says. He also claims that it's not as hot as you might imagine because the heat from the peppers is balanced by the burger's grease and the cheese.

"Craig's burgers blew our minds," says Brian. "They've got a taste that you remember."

Craig has been good for Brian's and Tyler's success as singers and songwriters as well. He championed the duo early on and is currently a partner in the Florida Georgia Line management company.

Brian's and Tyler's careers have skyrocketed, especially considering that they were unknown just a few years ago. They met while attending Belmont University in Nashville and instantly clicked. "We knew immediately," Tyler has said. "There's a solid foundation as friends between us. We're better together than apart, and that has always been easy for us."

They both knew they wanted to be musicians and set their paths accordingly—Tyler studied music business, while Brian chose entertainment industry studies. Music wasn't their only point of connection—they both came from small towns—Tyler from Monroe, Georgia, and Brian from Ormond Beach, Florida.

After college, they started working odd jobs during the day and slipping into songwriter sets at venues around Nashville at night. Growing up, they had both listened to a variety of music—everything from Garth Brooks' contemporary country to Eminem's hip-hop and Lynyrd Skynyrd's classic rock—and those influences seeped into their high-energy sound.

With Craig's help, they finally got a break—their debut album, *Here's to the Good Times*, reached number one on the country charts. In the last few years, Florida Georgia Line has been lauded with CMT, Academy of Country Music, and Country Music Association awards.

With all the success and traveling they do now, both Tyler and Brian admit they hardly cook at all. When they've got the rare evening back home in Nashville, Tyler might head out for a nice steak.

Brian, on the other hand, loves to just crash with a really good pizza, which when mentioned, reminds him that his dad back in Florida has become known for making homemade pizza from scratch and cooking it on the grill. Brian's dad might be at the ready to give the Florida Georgia Line duo some grilling pointers as well.

albums

Brian and Tyler's debut, *Here's to the Good Times*, reached number 1 on the country charts.

SERRANO PEPPER BURGERS

makes: 12 servings   hands-on time: 35 min.   total time: 1 hour

★ ★ ★

Since Brian and Tyler needed to improve their grilling skills, their famous songwriter friend Craig Wiseman shared his special recipe for these burgers with them. It's now one of their favorites.

★ ★ ★

1 lb. serrano peppers
2 Tbsp. olive oil
Sea salt
3 lb. ground chuck
Freshly ground black pepper
1 lb. pepper Jack cheese, sliced in ¼-inch slices

Butter
12 hamburger buns
Toppings: mustard, mayonnaise, ketchup, lettuce, tomato slices

1. Preheat one side of a grill to 350° to 400° (medium-high); leave other side unlit. Brush peppers with olive oil. Arrange peppers in a grill basket or on an aluminum foil tray over unlit side of grill, and grill, covered with grill lid, 10 to 15 minutes or until peppers begin to shrivel. Transfer peppers to lit side of grill, and grill, covered with grill lid, 8 to 10 minutes on each side or until lightly charred.

2. Remove peppers to a wire rack; cool to room temperature. Remove stems, slice in half lengthwise, and sprinkle with coarse salt.

3. Preheat unlit side of grill to 350° to 400° (medium-high). Shape meat evenly into 12 patties; sprinkle with salt and pepper. Grill patties 4 to 5 minutes on each side or until desired degree of doneness. Place 2 to 3 pepper halves over each patty; top evenly with cheese slices. Grill 1 to 2 minutes or until cheese melts.

4. Butter buns, and toast on grill. Serve patties on toasted buns with desired toppings—and get ready to enjoy a great burger!

☛ TIP ☚

You can substitute milder Anaheim peppers for the serranos if you prefer, but Craig says the fat in the burger and the milk in the cheese helps tamp down the hotness of the pepper. You can also serve the peppers alone as an appetizer with hoisin sauce or barbecue sauce.

WILD AT HEART • (KISSED YOU) GOOD NIGHT • Leave the Night

★ ★ WANNA TAKE YOU HOME • CAN'T SHAKE YOU ♪

How Far Do You Wanna Go? ★ ★ ★ THE WORLD
IS OURS TONIGHT ★ GOLD RUSH ★ Sunset Lovin'
• Carolina Rose • THE WAY IT GOES ★ ★
★ ★ ★ TURN MY WORLD AROUND ★ ★ Doing It Our Way ★ ★ ★

Where My Heart Belongs • IF YOU'RE LEAVIN' ♪ Soldier
Song • OVER ME NOW • You Said ★ ★ ★
★ ★ ★ COME AND SAVE ME • Change Your Mind ♪
Cry On Command • TIME TO LET ME GO •
★ ★ EVEN IF I WANTED TO ★ ★ ★ GO ON... MISS ME ★ ★
• All The Things That Mean The Most ♪

Gloriana

Brothers Tom and Mike Gossin found Rachel Reinert through her Myspace page, and they have been creating glorious harmonies ever since.

Tom and Mike Gossin took a circuitous route to Nashville. They grew up in a farmhouse in Utica, New York, where their dad worked as a truck driver for almost 30 years. Both of their parents were big music fans—the Nitty Gritty Dirt Band, Willie Nelson, and lots of Southern rock bands were among their favorites. "I remember waking up on Saturday and Sunday mornings to music blaring," says Mike. "It was like there was a soundtrack to every meal."

And meals in the Gossin house were big. Their mother went to culinary school and became a master at making desserts and pastries. "Every food she made was unbelievable," Mike adds.

The brothers both moved to Wilmington to attend the University of North Carolina. Eventually, they bailed on school and pursued music. They spent a decade playing clubs almost five nights a week before heading to Nashville. They borrowed their uncle's car, packed little more than a couple of acoustic guitars, and lit out.

The path for Rachel Reinert, Gloriana's third member, was just about as winding. She grew up in Sarasota, Florida, and later lived in Marietta, Georgia, and Santa Ana, California. Rachel started playing the guitar and writing poetry in school then began turning her poems into songs. She signed a publishing deal at age 16 and two years later moved to Nashville.

Tom and Mike were looking for a third voice to add to their band when they discovered Rachel's Myspace page. The three clicked immediately. "We knew we had something," says Mike. At the time, the brothers were in a desperate situation with no place to live. They all got along so well that eventually the brothers moved into a storage room in Rachel's one-bedroom apartment. "We never had the time or money to cook," recalls Mike. "It was the 'ramen noodles' type of thing."

They spent the next six months performing together and recorded a demo, which led to a deal and a debut album. The band's popularity took off. They won several "best new group" awards in their first year together. A few years later, their sophomore album featured the single "(Kissed You) Good Night," which went platinum.

These days, there's no longer a need to squeeze into a storage room. Tom and Mike have bought houses in the Nashville area, and Rachel has a condo downtown.

Mike loves the space he has now for cooking. One of his favorite warm-weather meals starts with Avocado and Feta Dip and includes Grilled Chicken and Fruit Summer Salad, which his health-conscious mom taught him how to make. Mike's such a fan of the dip, he jokes that he may have to write a song about it.

The band's heartier favorites include Beer-Can Chicken, done on the grill for minimum mess, and the spicy, juicy hunks of goodness they refer to as Pork Chops That Make You Crazy.

❧ albums & awards ❧

Tom and Mike Gossin and Rachel Reinert formed a band in 2008 with Cheyenne Kimball, (far left) on their self-titled album.

"(Kissed You) Good Night" reached the top 10 on country charts and the top 40 on pop charts.

Breakthrough Artist of the Year at the American Music Awards, 2009

CMT Nationwide on Your Side Award, 2009

Top New Vocal Group Award at the Academy of Country Music Awards, 2010

The band's breakout hit "(Kissed You) Good Night" went platinum.

MIKE GOSSIN SAYS THIS HEALTHY DIP IS ONE OF HIS FAVORITE THINGS HIS MOTHER MAKES. "I LIKE IT SO MUCH, I MAY HAVE TO WRITE A SONG ABOUT IT."

AVOCADO AND FETA DIP

makes: 10 to 12 appetizer servings (6 cups)
hands-on time: 25 min.   total time: 25 min.

- 1   lb. tomatoes on the vine, coarsely chopped
- 1   cup loosely packed fresh basil leaves, chopped
- 1   (8-oz.) pkg. feta cheese crumbles
- 3   medium avocados, cubed
- 2   Tbsp. olive oil
- 2   Tbsp. red wine vinegar
-     Table salt to taste
-     Freshly ground black pepper to taste
-     Tortilla chips

1. Toss together first 4 ingredients in a large bowl; set aside.

2. Whisk together olive oil and vinegar in a small bowl. Pour over avocado mixture, tossing to coat. Season with salt and pepper. Serve with tortilla chips.

★ ★ ★

Whether you call it a salsa or a dip, feta crumbles make this colorful, chunky avocado combo the perfect chip topper.

★ ★ ★

☞ TIP ☜

Feta can be pretty salty, so test for seasoning only after you've mixed everything else together. If people are dishing up rather than dipping, serve it with a slotted spoon because the feta and salt will draw juices out of the tomatoes.

AFTER "(KISSED YOU) GOOD NIGHT" REACHED THE TOP 10 ON COUNTRY CHARTS, DINNERS THAT FEATURED RAMEN NOODLES BECAME A DISTANT MEMORY FOR THE BAND.

GRILLED CHICKEN AND FRUIT SUMMER SALAD

makes: 4 servings   hands-on time: 35 min.
total time: 2 hours, 50 min.

Tom and Mike's mother learned a lot at culinary school, such as how to jazz up a summer lunch standby like chicken salad with juicy melon and crunchy pistachios.

¼   cup soy sauce
¼   cup honey
3   Tbsp. red wine vinegar
1   tsp. ground ginger
1   clove garlic, crushed
3   (4- to 6-oz.) boneless, skinless chicken breasts
1   head romaine lettuce, torn

1   apple, cubed
¾   cup diced cantaloupe
¾   cup diced honeydew melon
½   cup raisins
½   cup pistachios
1   cup reduced-fat honey-Dijon salad dressing

1. Whisk together soy sauce and next 4 ingredients in a small bowl. Place chicken in a large zip-top freezer bag; pour soy sauce mixture over chicken, turning to coat. Seal bag, and marinate in refrigerator 1 to 2 hours, turning occasionally.

2. Preheat grill to 350° to 400° (medium-high). Remove chicken from the marinade, discarding marinade in bag.

3. Grill chicken on lightly greased rack, covered with grill lid, 5 to 6 minutes on each side or until a meat thermometer inserted in the thickest part registers 165°. Remove chicken from grill; let stand 10 minutes. Slice chicken diagonally; set aside.

4. Combine romaine and next 5 ingredients in a large bowl. Top with chicken, and drizzle with salad dressing. Serve immediately.

BEER-CAN CHICKEN

makes: 4 servings **hands-on time: 20 min.** **total time: 2 hours**

1	Tbsp. smoked paprika		1	tsp. black pepper
1	Tbsp. table salt		1	tsp. garlic powder
1	Tbsp. onion powder		1	(4-lb.) chicken, rinsed and
1½	tsp. ground red pepper			patted dry
1½	tsp. ground cumin			Vegetable oil
1	tsp. dried thyme		1	(12-oz.) can beer
1	tsp. dried oregano			

1. Mix together smoked paprika and next 8 ingredients in a small bowl; set aside.

2. Preheat one side of grill to 350° to 400° (medium-high) heat; leave other side of grill unlit. Rub chicken and its cavity with vegetable oil and 1½ Tbsp. rub mixture. (Store extra rub in an airtight container up to 6 months, and you'll have it on hand for the next chicken!)

3. Open beer. Have a sip or pour a few tablespoons out. Place chicken upright onto beer can, fitting can into cavity. Pull legs forward to form a tripod, allowing chicken to stand upright. Place the chicken over unlit side of the grill.

4. Grill, covered with grill lid, 1 to 1½ hours or until golden and an instant-read thermometer inserted in thigh registers 180°. Carefully remove beer can. Cover chicken loosely with aluminum foil; let rest 10 minutes before cutting into quarters.

★ ★ ★

This chicken grills up moist, delicious, and mostly unattended while you—and the bird—kick back with a cold one.

★ ★ ★

 **TIP**

Be extra careful when you remove the beer can—it will be hot!

THE BAND IS ESPECIALLY PROUD OF THEIR COOKING SKILLS THESE DAYS. THE PORK CHOPS—SPICY, JUICY, HUNKS OF GOODNESS—HAVE BEEN KNOWN TO INDUCE TEMPORARY INSANITY.

PORK CHOPS THAT MAKE YOU CRAZY

makes: 8 servings   hands-on time: 15 min.   total time: 35 min.

★ ★ ★

The triple threat of red, white, and black pepper in the dredge is the secret to these flavorful chops.

★ ★ ★

$^1/_2$ cup all-purpose flour	$^1/_2$ tsp. garlic powder
2 tsp. table salt	$^1/_2$ tsp. dried thyme
2 tsp. paprika	$^1/_2$ tsp. ground red pepper
1 tsp. black pepper	8 center-cut bone-in pork
$^3/_4$ tsp. white pepper	chops, (about 3 to 3 $^1/_2$ lbs.)
$^3/_4$ tsp. onion powder	2 Tbsp. vegetable oil, divided

1. Whisk together flour and next 8 ingredients in a large shallow bowl. Dredge half of the pork chops in flour mixture; shake off excess, and set aside.

2. Heat 1 Tbsp. oil in a large nonstick skillet over medium-high heat just until smoking. Cook chops in hot oil 5 minutes or until golden, turning once. Reduce heat to medium; cook 2 minutes, turning once. Transfer chops to plate, and keep warm.

3. Repeat process with remaining oil and chops.

FRENCH TOAST BAKE WITH SAUSAGE

makes: **8 to 10 servings**   hands-on time: **25 min.**
total time: **9 hours, 30 min., including chilling**

★ ★ ★

Meals in the Gossin house were big, including this easy breakfast casserole. Sweet, savory, and creamy, it hits every note. Best of all, you assemble it the night before, and just pop it in the oven in the morning.

★ ★ ★

1   (9.6-oz.) package fully cooked pork or turkey sausage links, sliced ¼-inch thick
8   slices thick-sliced white bread, cubed
2   (8-oz.) pkgs. cream cheese, cubed
12 eggs, lightly beaten
2   cups milk
½   cup maple syrup
1   tsp. vanilla extract
½   tsp. ground cinnamon
Warm maple syrup (optional)

1. Heat sausage slices according to package directions; set aside.

2. Arrange half of bread cubes in a lightly greased 13- x 9-inch baking dish. Arrange cream cheese over bread cubes. Top with remaining bread cubes. Sprinkle sausage slices over top.

3. Whisk together eggs, milk, maple syrup, vanilla, and cinnamon. Pour over top; cover and chill 8 hours.

4. Preheat oven to 375°. Bake at 375° for 45 minutes. Serve with warm maple syrup, if desired.

TIP

To quickly and easily cut cream cheese into cubes, freeze it for 15 to 20 minutes, and then cut it with a wire cheese slicer.

Amy Grant

When she's not writing songs, performing, or joining husband Vince Gill on tour, Amy Grant riffs on pot roast and banana bread in her Nashville kitchen, where comfort foods take center stage.

Amy Grant has great reverence for a speckled blue roasting pan that sits in her pantry. It belonged to her husband Vince Gill's grandmother—a legendary cook. "That pan has been reason enough for me to perfect my pot roast recipe," says the singer-songwriter. And perfect it she has. After a helpful tip from Vince's mother, Jerene, to sear the beef before placing it in the roaster, Amy now thinks she has a pretty good thing going.

In her Amy's Pot Roast recipe, she includes her own helpful tip right off the bat: "Do not take a shower before you start this process because you will definitely need one when you are finished." The combination of the meat and the garlic all cause one to walk away smelling like a seared roast. "I always cook that pot roast recipe because it is extraordinary," she says. She thinks it's great for feeding a lot of people—at church potlucks or when there's a death in a family. "It's not sexy, but it's comfort food."

Having grown up in Nashville, Amy has been performing professionally since she was 16 years old. She has sold more than 30 million albums and still keeps an active tour schedule, sometimes performing with Vince on the road.

When she and Vince met in the mid 1990s, she was considered the iconic voice of Christian pop, and he was one of the most popular acts in country music. They were singing a duet together for her album

House of Love, and when they got together to tape the video, they immediately connected.

"I felt like I knew him instantly," she has said in an interview. "I was so moved by him as a human being that I went up behind him and just hugged him as hard as I could while he was singing." Both Amy and Vince were married at the time, and they stayed faithful to their spouses, but eventually they followed their hearts. They wed in 2000, blending their families. Vince had a daughter, Amy had a son and two daughters, and they had a daughter together.

"One of the ways I get grounded again after being on the road is to cook," Amy says. "I love to cook because it's creative. You can have a recipe, but you can always add and subtract and make it your own." Her mother was always cooking for Amy and her three sisters. She prepared a hot breakfast every morning and made sure that the family was sitting around the table every night for dinner. As adults, they always returned home for Thanksgiving dinner. After Amy's mother passed away a few years ago, the sisters decided to make Easter dinner their family tradition instead.

At their home in Nashville, Amy and Vince and their children have a holiday dinner tradition as well. On Christmas Eve, the kids handle the meal—from cooking to setting the table and washing up. "We have an amazing meal, and the kids do it all," Amy says. "Even better, they really enjoy doing it."

❧ albums & awards ❧

Amy is the best-selling contemporary Christian singer ever.

Amy Grant won six Grammys between 1982 and 2006.

She was inducted into the Gospel Music Hall of Fame in 2003, and has won 25 Dove Awards.

In 2005, she was awarded a star on the Hollywood Walk of Fame.

"I accidentally ended up in the music business," writes Amy in *Mosaic: Pieces of My Life So Far.*

"DO NOT TAKE A SHOWER BEFORE YOU START THIS PROCESS BECAUSE YOU WILL DEFINITELY NEED ONE WHEN YOU ARE FINISHED."

AMY'S POT ROAST

makes: 8 to 10 servings   hands-on time: 40 min.
total time: 5 hours, 40 min.

★ ★ ★

Amy loves to make this dish on a day she knows she'll be staying home to enjoy it. She says Vince hates onions but doesn't mind these because they cook away to nothing and leave a natural sweetness.

★ ★ ★

2   (3-lb.) beef chuck roasts
3   Tbsp. Montreal-style steak seasoning
1/4   cup olive oil
4   medium-size yellow onions, quartered
4   (14-oz.) cans beef broth, divided
1   cup dry red wine
4   garlic cloves, minced
1 1/2   tsp. table salt
1/2   tsp. freshly ground black pepper
1   (10 3/4-oz.) can cream of mushroom soup
3   Tbsp. maple syrup
1   (16-oz.) bag baby carrots
1   (28-oz.) bag baby red potatoes
Garnish: fresh parsley sprigs

1. Preheat oven to 400°. Sprinkle roasts on all sides with Montreal seasoning. Cook roasts, one at a time, in 2 Tbsp. hot oil in a Dutch oven about 15 minutes, turning to brown meat on all sides.

2. Arrange onions in bottom of a large roasting pan.

3. Top with roasts, and add 3 cans of beef broth or enough to partially cover roasts by two-thirds.

4. Whisk together wine and next 3 ingredients in a small bowl; pour over beef. Bake, covered, at 400° for 4 hours or until meat is tender and pulls apart easily.

5. Whisk together remaining beef broth, soup, and maple syrup in a medium bowl; pour over beef. Add carrots and potatoes to roasting pan; cover and bake 1 hour or until vegetables are tender. Let stand 10 minutes before serving.

"ONE OF THE WAYS I GET GROUNDED AGAIN AFTER BEING ON THE ROAD IS TO GET IN THE KITCHEN AND COOK. I LOVE TO COOK BECAUSE IT'S CREATIVE."

BANANA NUT BREAD

makes: 1 loaf (10 to 12 servings)   **hands-on time: 20 min.**
total time: 2 hours, 20 min.

½   cup butter, softened
1   cup sugar
2   large eggs
2   cups all-purpose flour
1   tsp. baking soda

Dash of table salt
4   small bananas, sliced
     (about 2 cups)
½   cup coarsely chopped
     toasted pecans

1. Beat butter at medium speed with an electric mixer until creamy. Gradually add sugar, beating until light and fluffy. Add eggs, 1 at a time, beating just until blended after each addition.

2. Combine flour and next 2 ingredients; gradually add to butter mixture, beating at low speed just until blended. Stir in bananas and pecans. Spoon batter into a greased and floured 9- x 5-inch loaf pan.

3. Place pan in a cold oven. Set oven to 300°. Bake for 1 hour and 20 minutes or until a long wooden pick inserted in center comes out clean and sides pull away from the pan. Shield bread with aluminum foil after 1 hour to prevent browning, if necessary. Cool bread in pan on a wire rack 10 minutes; remove from pan, and cool 30 minutes on wire rack before slicing.

★ ★ ★

This Grant-Gill family staple is the perfect way to use up any old bananas you might have in the house.

★ ★ ★

☞ TIP ☜

If you don't have overripe bananas, arrange them (skin on) on a baking sheet, and bake at 300° for 1 hour. Then place them in the refrigerator for 15 minutes or until they are cool enough to slice.

COUNTRY MUSIC'S GREATEST EATS

Kree Harrison

Kree Harrison's run to runner-up on *American Idol* launched her career, but she's been singing country, R&B, and religious music since she was a young girl. Born in Texas, Kree grew up close enough to Cajun country to absorb its unique culture.

When you are raised not far from the Texas-Louisiana border, Mom's Gumbo at the holidays rings just as true as a turkey or a ham, and a pan full of dressing.

This is the case for country singer Kree Harrison, who says her mother always celebrated Cajun Christmases when they lived in Woodville, Texas, which is near Lake Charles, Louisiana. What made it special was her mother's perfect roux.

Kree also remembers eating crawfish and Cajun boudin (a sausage casing stuffed with a pork and rice dressing and then steamed or grilled) and the abundance of seasonings. "Everybody puts Tony Chachere's on everything," she says with a laugh.

Not only can you taste the Cajun influence, but you can hear it, too. Zydeco music drifted through their house and is very much an element of Kree's own musical style. She once opened for Wayne Toups, one of the most successful Cajun and Zydeco singers and songwriters, best known for his dynamic accordion playing. "The Cajun roots are definitely there," she says.

But Kree came to love lots of different kinds of music, even at a very early age. At 8, she opened for Percy Sledge (the R&B artist famous for the song "When a Man Loves a Woman"). She also sang religious songs in church and country songs at various venues in the area.

Country music seemed to be her calling, though, and after Kree completed fifth grade, her family moved to Nashville in hopes of launching her career. Sadly, not long after moving, her father died in a plane crash, and a few years later, her mother was tragically killed in a car accident.

With her family's support and encouragement, Kree kept on singing and writing, playing gigs and working with other songwriters. In early 2013, she auditioned and landed a spot on the TV show *American Idol*. She was a strong contender the entire season and finished as the runner-up, which took her career to the next level.

Now that she's on tour so much, she says that seafood reminds her of home and very happy memories. Her dad liked to make fried shrimp, and he included a secret special seasoning in the batter. "Anytime I have that, I think of him," she says.

Not surprisingly, she says she's nearly always open to trying gumbo when it's on the menu. "But it's not as good as what I'm used to," she says. Her mother's recipe goes back some generations in the family. "It's such a wonderful tradition that I'm trying my best to carry it on," she says. "If my mother taught me anything, it's that it's all about the roux."

albums & awards

In 2013, Kree was the runner-up on the 12th season of *American Idol*.

Kree has been singing for most of her life. When she was 8 years old, she opened for R&B legend Percy Sledge.

KREE'S MOTHER'S GUMBO RECIPE CAME FROM HER GRANDMOTHER AND GOES BACK SOME GENERATIONS. **"IF MY MOTHER TAUGHT ME ANYTHING, IT'S THAT IT'S ALL ABOUT THE ROUX."**

MOM'S GUMBO

makes: 10 to 12 servings (18 cups)   hands-on time: 1 hour, 5 min.
total time: 2 hours, 35 min.

★ ★ ★

This recipe is very special to Kree. She got it from her late mother, who was greatly influenced by Cajun dishes. In addition to making the roux from scratch, she didn't shy away from adding spice and hot sauce.

★ ★ ★

2   extra-large chicken bouillon cubes
1   large yellow onion, chopped
1½   cups chopped green onions
1   cup chopped celery
1   green bell pepper, chopped
1½   cups prepared dark roux*
12   chicken legs (about 4 lb.)
6   chicken thighs (about 2½ lb.)
Table salt to taste
Freshly ground black pepper to taste
Garlic powder
Cajun seasoning
2   Tbsp. vegetable oil
2   (16-oz.) packages andouille or smoked sausage, sliced
½   tsp. filé powder
Hot sauce (optional)
9   cups hot cooked rice

1. Combine bouillon cubes and 16 cups water in a large Dutch oven, and bring to a boil over high heat. Add chopped onions, celery, and bell pepper; reduce heat, and cook over medium-high heat 20 minutes. Return mixture to a boil, add roux, and cook, stirring occasionally, 30 minutes or until thickened.

2. Season chicken liberally with salt and next 3 ingredients. Cook chicken, in batches, in hot oil in a large skillet over medium heat 2 minutes on each side or until golden. Remove chicken from skillet; drain on paper towels.

3. Add chicken and sausage to roux mixture; reduce heat, and cook over low heat, stirring occasionally, 1 hour. Remove from heat. Skim fat from top of soup.

4. Remove chicken from soup; cool to room temperature. Skin, bone, and coarsely chop chicken; add meat to soup. Stir in filé powder and hot sauce, if desired. Serve over hot cooked rice.

*You may use ¾ of a (16-oz.) jar of prepared roux (such as Savoie's Old Fashioned Dark Roux) or make your own roux by whisking 1¼ cups flour into 1¼ cups melted butter or vegetable oil, and cooking the mixture over medium heat, stirring occasionally, until it's the desired color—a deep dark brown.

The Henningsens

This father-daughter-son trio kicked off their careers writing songs for other artists. Now that The Henningsens are enjoying their own success on the road, their family bond has never been stronger.

Listen to a few tracks by The Henningsens, and there's no mistaking the kinship of this family band. Clara's fresh voice opens most of the songs—upbeat tunes that edge toward bluegrass telling the stories of characters and relationships—before her father, Brian, and brother Aaron join to complete a soothing harmony. "We try to be very lyrically descriptive," says Brian. "We always say it when we write—we're trying to make a little movie play in your mind. If you can touch somebody emotionally and say something that's actually worth saying, then you've done your job as a songwriter and an artist."

It's a pattern that has served them well. The band found their footing in Nashville writing songs for others, including Wynonna Judd, Sara Evans, Highway 101, and The Band Perry. But in 2013, they finally released an EP, etching a name for themselves and truly stepping into their own as a band.

Yes, they are a band, but they are also a dad and his kids, and Clara notes that the dynamic has been healthy and interesting to navigate. "Obviously there are times when he's our dad, and he knows best," she explains, "but we're in a partnership together, so we talk to come to a final decision. We have to work things out together."

To understand The Henningsens the band, you must know the story about The Henningsens the family—10 children—10 children!—and a mom and a dad, who still manage a 1,700-acre corn and soybean farm in Atwood, Illinois, that has been in the family for seven generations.

"My parents say they never planned on having 10 kids, but it was pretty much free farm labor," Clara remarks with a laugh. Three families of cousins lived nearby, so there was never any down time.

Growing up on a farm fostered Clara's love of gardening. "It's one of my favorite things to do," she

"If you can touch somebody emotionally and say something that's actually worth saying, then you've done your job as a songwriter and an artist," Brian says. "And that's really our biggest goal."

says. She remembers picking rhubarb for her mother, Debby, to make her Honey-Rhubarb Pie which became a hit. Another favorite, especially among the kids, is her mother's Honey Chicken, fried chicken tenders with a garlicky honey dipping sauce.

As Clara watched her father and grandfather harvest the crops on the farm, she learned the importance of a strong work ethic. "They taught me that when life seems impossible, you've got to keep going."

Clara adds that she thinks about that lesson almost every day in the music business. It's a business that she and her siblings have been around for most of their lives. "We've always been musical, but we didn't grow up like the von Trapps!"

Clara explains that her father performed in a Christian band and pursued a solo artist career in the 1990s. He was beginning to make some traction in Nashville when his father was seriously injured in a farm accident, and Brian set his music dream aside for a while to keep the farming operation going. Around 2007, Brian, Clara, and Aaron began to get serious about singing and writing together. The more they performed, the more their fan base grew. "Many people came up to us saying, 'I would do anything to play music with my dad or brother,'" Clara recalls. "We realized how cool it was to get to share this journey together."

Several years ago, Brian and Debby—who had developed an affinity for the South and the state of Tennessee—bought an 80-acre farm outside Nashville. "It was like an adventure," says Clara. "Everytime we would go, we were going to work on the house and the land. That got us used to coming down South." When the band isn't touring, the Henningsens split their time between the new Nashville farm and the old homestead farm back in Illinois.

(continued on page 147)

"MANY PEOPLE CAME UP TO US SAYING, 'I WOULD DO ANYTHING TO PLAY MUSIC WITH MY DAD OR BROTHER,'" CLARA RECALLS. "WE REALIZED HOW COOL IT WAS TO GET TO SHARE THIS JOURNEY TOGETHER.

Aaron and Clara now have their own places in Nashville. Like her mother, Clara enjoys cooking. She and her husband, Jacob Calaway, like to grill together, especially venison, mahi-mahi, and grouper, and they're slowly developing their own favorite family recipes. Cooking is "definitely still a huge part of my life and who I am," she notes.

The Henningsens enjoy their time together, whether it's over a glass of milk at the bar *(at left)* or picking up their instruments for a spontaneous jam session *(below)*.

albums

The Henningsens began their music career writing songs that were later recorded by artists such as Wynonna Judd, Sara Evans, and the band Highway 101.

"American Beautiful," the first single featuring The Henningsens as performers, was released in 2012.

LIKE HER MOTHER, CLARA ENJOYS COOKING. "IT'S DEFINITELY STILL A HUGE PART OF MY LIFE AND WHO I AM."

These sweet-batter fried chicken tenders, served with the honey and garlic dipping sauce, are a Henningsen family favorite.

HONEY CHICKEN

makes: 4 to 6 servings   hands-on time: 35 min.
total time: 40 min., including the sauce

1½	lb. skinned and boned chicken breasts	¼	tsp. freshly ground black pepper
1	cup all-purpose flour	¼	tsp. garlic powder
1½	tsp. baking powder	2	cups canola oil
½	tsp. table salt		

1. Cut chicken into 1½- x 5-inch strips or into about 48 (1½-inch) cubes.

2. Whisk together flour and next 4 ingredients. Whisk in ¾ to 1 cup of water or enough water to form a slightly runny batter.

3. Pour canola oil to a depth of ½ inch in a large deep skillet; heat to 350°.

4. Dip chicken in flour mixture. Fry chicken, in batches, in hot oil 2 to 3 minutes on each side or until done and golden brown. Drain on paper towels. Serve with Honey Sauce.

HONEY SAUCE

makes: ½ cup   hands-on time: 4 min.   total time: 4 min.

½	cup honey	2	garlic cloves, minced
½	tsp. soy sauce		

1. Combine all ingredients in a small saucepan, and cook over low heat for 4 to 6 minutes.

"MY FAMILY ALWAYS HAD A BIG PATCH OF RHUBARB IN THE GARDEN WHEN I WAS GROWING UP THAT WAS PROBABLY PLANTED BY MY GREAT-GREAT-GRANDMOTHER,**"** SAYS CLARA.

HONEY-RHUBARB PIE

makes: 8 servings   **hands-on time: 35 min.**
total time: 3 hours, 5 min.

1¼ cups sugar	5 drops red food coloring
6 Tbsp. all-purpose flour	1 (14.1-oz.) package
2 tsp. lemon zest	refrigerated piecrusts
¼ tsp. table salt	2 Tbsp. butter
4 cups chopped fresh rhubarb	1 Tbsp. milk
⅓ cup honey	Sugar for sprinkling

1. Preheat oven to 400°. Whisk together 1¼ cups sugar and next 3 ingredients in a large bowl; stir in rhubarb.

2. Whisk together honey and food coloring in a small bowl; stir into rhubarb mixture.

3. Fit 1 piecrust into a 9-inch pie plate according to package directions. Trim off excess pastry along edges of pie plate. Spoon rhubarb mixture into crust, mounding in center; dot with butter. Place remaining piecrust over rhubarb mixture, fold edges under, sealing to bottom crust, and crimp. Brush top of pie, excluding fluted edges, with milk; sprinkle lightly with sugar. Place pie on a jelly-roll pan. Cut 4 or 5 slits in top of pie for steam to escape.

4. Bake at 400° for 50 minutes, shielding the edges with aluminum foil after 15 minutes to prevent excessive browning. Remove to a wire rack. Cool 1½ to 2 hours before serving.

★ ★ ★

Fresh rhubarb translates into some fresh, delicious Honey-Rhubarb Pie, which never lasts long at the Henningsen house.

★ ★ ★

Alan Jackson

Food has played such an important role in the life of legendary country music singer-songwriter Alan Jackson that he wrote a cookbook to celebrate his favorite family meals.

Alan Jackson first met his wife, Denise, when she was working at a Dairy Queen in Newnan, Georgia. They were both in high school, and they soon became sweethearts.

Newnan sits not too far off Interstate 85 about 35 miles southwest of Atlanta, and it is one of the fastest growing cities in the state. But when Alan was coming of age there in the 1960s and 1970s, the town was much smaller and simpler. He grew up in an old frame house with a dirt driveway, willow trees, and a small garden. And his mother, Ruth, cooked all the time, preparing lots of classic Southern dishes for Alan and his family, which included four older sisters.

This was a house where creamy mashed potatoes could always find a new, battered-and-fried life with his mother's Leftover Mashed Potato Cakes. Simple dishes are still Alan's favorites. He's been known to pass up elaborate spreads for a bowl of beans and cornbread. He alludes to the simplicity and slower pace of his origin in his song "Where I Come From:" "Where I come from/It's cornbread and chicken/Where I come from a lotta front porch sittin'/Where I come from tryin' to make a livin'/And workin' hard to get to heaven."

Alan has never been a stranger to hard work. At 12, he took a job at a shoe repair shop. Later, he sold cars and furniture and attempted carpentry and building houses. He even drove a forklift at a K-Mart, and when he moved to Nashville to pursue his music career, he landed a job in the mailroom of The Nashville Network (TNN) television station. "If I want to try to do something, I do it. I've never really been afraid of failure," he says on his website, www.alanjackson.com.

Alan was certainly trying and working hard, but actually it was his wife, Denise, who got him his big break. She met country singer Glen Campbell in an airport, and she just happened to be carrying one of Alan's tapes. She shared it with Glen, Glen gave her his card, and pretty soon Alan was signing a record deal.

Long after "Alan Jackson" became a household name, he wrote a cookbook called *Who Says You Can't Cook It All*, available on his website. Named for his song "(Who Says) You Can't Have It All" and updated in 2009, the cookbook features 60 of Alan's delicious family recipes.

Food has been there since the beginning for Alan and Denise. We don't know for sure what he ordered the day he met her (it was likely sweet—one of his favorite "meals" is a pineapple and Blue Plate-brand mayonnaise sandwich). We do know he mustered the courage to talk to her. And after 30 years of marriage, raising three daughters, and a successful career, Alan continues living with a pretty simple mantra: "You've got to live life. You've got to get out there and do it," he emphasizes. "Time's wastin'."

albums & awards

Country music singer and songwriter Alan Jackson has had at least 35 number one hits on the country charts.

He's sold more than 60 million records worldwide.

To date, he has won 17 Country Music Association awards, two Grammys, and 16 Academy of Country Music awards.

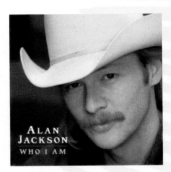

Alan's 1994 album *Who I Am* featured four number one songs, including "Livin' on Love" and "Gone Country."

COUNTRY MUSIC'S GREATEST EATS

ALAN NAMED HIS COOKBOOK, *WHO SAYS YOU CAN'T COOK IT ALL,* **AFTER HIS HIT** "(WHO SAYS) YOU CAN'T HAVE IT ALL."

ALAN'S FAVORITE CHICKEN SALAD

makes: 6 servings   **hands-on time: 25 min.**
total time: 1 hour, 20 min.

★ ★ ★

This chicken salad caters to Alan's sweet tooth (one of his favorite meals is a pineapple and Blue Plate-brand mayonnaise sandwich). This recipe includes both pineapple juice and honey. Ain't that sweet?

★ ★ ★

4 (6-oz.) skinned and boned chicken breasts
1 (46-oz.) can pineapple juice
2 Tbsp. honey
1 tsp. apple cider vinegar
½ cup toasted slivered almonds
¾ cup mayonnaise
1 cup sweetened dried cranberries (optional)
Sea salt to taste
Freshly ground black pepper to taste
Lettuce leaves

1. Bring chicken and next 3 ingredients to a light boil in a large Dutch oven over medium heat; reduce heat to medium-low, cover, and simmer 45 minutes or until chicken is tender. Remove from heat; drain. Cool chicken 10 minutes; shred chicken with two forks.

2. Combine chicken, almonds, mayonnaise, and cranberries, if desired, in a large bowl. Add salt and pepper. Serve on lettuce leaves.

MAMA RUTH'S LEFTOVER MASHED POTATO CAKES

makes: 4 servings   **hands-on time: 25 min.**   **total time: 1 hour**

★ ★ ★

These fried mashed potato cakes are a perfect way to extend the goodness of creamy, leftover mashed potatoes.

★ ★ ★

2 cups prepared mashed potatoes, chilled
1 large egg, lightly beaten
½ cup all-purpose flour, divided
¾ cup vegetable oil
Table salt to taste

1. Combine potatoes, egg, and 2 Tbsp. flour in a large bowl; cover and chill 30 minutes.

2. Preheat oven to 200°. Place remaining flour in a large shallow bowl. Shape potato mixture into 8 (3- x ½-inch) patties. Dredge patties in flour; shake off excess flour.

3. Fry patties, in 2 batches, in hot oil about ¼-inch deep in a large skillet over medium-high heat for 1 to 1½ minutes on each side or until browned. Place patties on a wire rack over a jelly-roll pan; place in preheated oven to keep warm. Repeat process with remaining patties. Season before serving.

ALAN'S MOTHER PREPARED LOTS OF CLASSIC SOUTHERN DISHES FOR ALAN AND HIS FOUR SISTERS. SIMPLE DISHES ARE STILL HIS FAVORITE.

ALAN'S PHILLY CHEESE CHICKEN SANDWICHES

makes: 4 servings   hands-on time: 20 min.   total time: 45 min.

4 (6-oz.) skinned and boned chicken breasts	1 medium-size green bell pepper, sliced
1 tsp. Southwest seasoning	1 small onion, sliced
Table salt to taste	4 sourdough bread slices
Freshly ground black pepper to taste	1 (8-oz.) package shredded pepper Jack cheese

1. Preheat oven to 350°. Sprinkle chicken breasts with desired amount of Southwest seasoning, salt, and pepper.

2. Brown chicken breasts in a large skillet coated with vegetable cooking spray over medium heat 5 minutes on each side. Remove chicken from skillet, cool 10 minutes, and shred meat with 2 forks. Set aside, and keep warm.

3. Cook bell pepper and onion slices in skillet over medium heat until soft and browned, stirring often. Add 4 to 6 Tbsp. water, 1 Tbsp. at a time, to prevent vegetables from sticking. Add shredded chicken to skillet; cover, reduce heat to medium-low, and cook until heated through.

4. Arrange bread slices on baking sheet, sprinkle evenly with half of cheese. Bake at 350° for 4 to 5 minutes or cheese melts; increase oven temperature to broil. Remove toast from oven; top with chicken mixture and remaining cheese. Broil toast 5 to 7 minutes or until golden and cheese melts. Serve open-faced sandwiches immediately.

NOTE: We tested with Emeril's Southwest Essence.

★ ★ ★

This chicken version of a Philly cheese steak sandwich is great for lunch. Add coleslaw and chips, then top it all off with a slice of pie for dessert.

★ ★ ★

DENISE'S FAVORITE GERMAN CHOCOLATE CAKE

makes: 12 servings   hands-on time: 1 hour
total time: 2 hours, 45 min.

★ ★ ★

Alan Jackson's wife, Denise, makes this fabulous cake. Don't lick the frosting spoon too much—the recipe makes just enough to spread between the layers and cover the top and sides of the cake.

★ ★ ★

Wax paper
1   (4-oz.) package sweet chocolate baking bars
2   cups all-purpose flour
1   tsp. baking soda
¼   tsp. sea salt

1   cup butter, softened
2   cups sugar
4   large eggs, separated
1   tsp. vanilla extract
1   cup buttermilk
Coconut-Pecan Frosting

1. Preheat oven to 350°. Lightly grease 3 (9-inch) round cake pans. Line bottoms of pans with wax paper.

2. Microwave chocolate and ½ cup water in a microwave-safe glass bowl at HIGH for 1 to 1½ minutes or until chocolate melts and is smooth, stirring once halfway through. Combine flour and next 2 ingredients in a medium bowl.

3. Beat butter and sugar at medium speed with an electric mixer until fluffy. Add egg yolks, 1 at a time, beating until just blended after each addition. Stir in chocolate mixture and vanilla. Add flour mixture alternately with buttermilk, beginning and ending with flour mixture. Beat at low speed until just blended after each addition.

4. Beat egg whites at high speed until stiff peaks form; gently fold into batter. Pour batter into prepared pans. Bake at 350° for 25 to 30 minutes or until a wooden pick inserted in center comes out clean. Remove from oven, and gently run a knife around outer edge of cake layers. Cool on wire racks 15 minutes. Remove from pans to wire racks; discard wax paper. Cool completely (about 1 hour). Spread Coconut-Pecan Frosting between layers and on top and sides of cake.

NOTE: We tested with Baker's German's Sweet Chocolate Bar.

COCONUT-PECAN FROSTING

1   (12-oz.) can evaporated milk
1½   cups sugar
¾   cup butter
4   large egg yolks, lightly beaten

2⅔   cups sweetened flaked coconut
1½   cups chopped toasted pecans
1½   tsp. vanilla extract

1. Combine milk and next 3 ingredients in a large saucepan over medium heat, stirring constantly, 3 to 4 minutes or until butter melts and sugar dissolves. Cook, stirring constantly, 12 to 14 minutes or until mixture becomes a light caramel color, bubbles, and reaches a pudding-like thickness.

2. Remove pan from heat; stir in coconut, pecans and vanilla. Transfer mixture to a bowl. Let stand, stirring occasionally, 45 minutes or until cool and spreading consistency.

Casey James

Affable singer-songwriter Casey James infuses his country music with bluesy rock and Texas cool. The laidback musician with the long wavy locks has a busy touring schedule, so when he's home, he appreciates having time to cook.

Casey James will make you believe in fate. Or predestination. Or the idea that some force in the universe ushers us to the right path to walk, the right door to open. For starters, he grew up in (no joke) Cool, Texas, a dot on the map roughly 45 miles west of Fort Worth.

Casey's family is musical. Both his parents sing, and his dad plays the guitar. One of his earliest memories is listening to a Ricky Skaggs album at his grandparents' house when he was 4 years old. "'Walking in Jerusalem' has this guitar intro, and then the drums and bass come in," he recalls. "I remember moving a chair over in front of the speakers, just sitting there and listening, and as soon as all the instruments came in, I would start the song over." And over and over and over, until his grandmother finally made him stop.

That was the right path. Casey's mother bought him his first guitar when he was 13 years old. "I've sung my whole life, but I feel a lot closer to the guitar because I had to really work at it as a craft," he explains. "Once I learned to play, I fell in love with the ability to make music, to put my fingers on the strings and make a beautiful song."

His musical interests were varied and ever evolving. He cut his teeth on the traditional country stars—Merle Haggard and George Jones—before moving on to more contemporary artists such as George Strait and Garth Brooks. Then came classic rock, Seattle grunge, and the bluesy riffs of fellow Texan Stevie Ray Vaughn and the blues masters of the Mississippi Delta.

albums & awards

Casey James competed in and placed third in the ninth season of *American Idol*, which aired in 2010.

His self-titled debut album was released in 2012.

That confluence of styles molded Casey, and by 17, he was singing for money, booking birthday parties and performing in restaurant corners or on small club stages. Four years later, a serious motorcycle accident left him with near-career-ending wrist and arm injuries. Months of recovery and rehabilitation followed. Rather than deterring his passion for music, the setback gave him a broader perspective, and he began to play again.

At his mother's insistence, Casey auditioned for the ninth season of *American Idol*, which aired in 2010. He brought his soulful style to the stage, drawing on his blues and rock guitar skills, and it earned him third place in the competition and, more importantly, a record deal. Casey has spent the last few years touring all over the country, opening for bands such as Sugarland and artists including Taylor Swift. While on the road, Casey "rarely" has the opportunity to cook, something he says he has enjoyed since he was young.

And though his career seems almost preordained, Casey remains grounded and humble and focused on doing what he loves. "If you want to be famous, you're asking the wrong person," he says. "Being famous means nothing to me. It doesn't do me any good. What does mean something is doing what I love to do. I'm always gonna play music, whether that's for 10 people in a smoky bar, millions of viewers on *American Idol*, or 50,000 people in a stadium someday, if I'm ever that lucky."

" I COULD EAT SUSHI EVERY DAY, AND SALMON IS ONE OF MY FAVORITE FOODS. THIS SALMON IS BOTH SWEET AND SPICY, AND I LIKE THE CRUNCH OF THE CHOPPED NUTS ON TOP. "

CHUCK "THE YANK'S" WORLD-FAMOUS BBQ SALMON

**makes: 4 servings   hands-on time: 30 min.
total time: 2 hours, 5 min.**

★ ★ ★

Chuck "The Yank" is a James family friend who also happens to make Casey's favorite salmon recipe. A charcoal kettle-style grill is ideal for making it because the grill grate easily spins in the kettle. You don't have to use a spatula and risk mangling the fish—just rotate the grate to move the fish to the unlit side.

★ ★ ★

1½	cups apple wood chips	1	Tbsp. lemon pepper
Half of 1 sweet onion, pureed (about ½ cup)		1	tsp. kosher salt
		½	tsp. ground red pepper
4	garlic cloves, chopped	½	cup triple sec
½	cup melted butter	3	Tbsp. fresh lemon juice
2	Tbsp. olive oil	1	Tbsp. Worcestershire sauce
½	cup firmly packed dark brown sugar	¾	cup chopped toasted slivered almonds
1	Tbsp. dry mustard	1½	lbs. skinless salmon fillets, cut in 12-oz. portions
1	Tbsp. paprika		

1. Soak wood chips in water to cover.

2. Cook onion puree and garlic in butter and hot oil in a skillet over medium-high heat 2 to 3 minutes or until lightly browned. Stir in brown sugar and next 8 ingredients, and bring to a boil. Reduce heat, and simmer over medium-low heat, stirring often, 2 minutes or until mixture begins to thicken. Stir in almonds, and remove from heat. Transfer mixture to a 2-quart glass baking dish; cool 10 minutes. Place salmon in almond mixture, turning to coat; cover and let stand 30 minutes.

3. Drain wood chips, and wrap in aluminum foil, leaving ends of foil packet open. Light one side of grill, and heat to 400° to 500° (high); leave other side of grill unlit. Lay foil packet along inside edge of grill, directly over flame. Cover with grill lid for 20 minutes.

4. Place salmon on lightly oiled grill rack over lit side of grill, and grill, covered with grill lid, 2 minutes, without turning. Transfer fillets to unlit side of grill; spoon any remaining sauce over top of each fillet. Grill, covered with grill lid without turning, 10 minutes, or to desired degree of doneness.

5. Cut fillets in half, and serve immediately.

Wynonna Judd

Wynonna Judd and her mother, Naomi, dominated the country music stage for nearly 10 years before Wynonna went solo. These days, she is passing on to her daughter, Grace, the lessons—and recipes—she learned from the women in her family.

Wynonna Judd associates comfort and healing with her recipe for Grace's Favorite Broccoli-Rice Casserole. "Grace will always come to me in her hour of need and say she wants the casserole," the singer says about her 18-year-old daughter. "It won't make her life complete, but for that moment in time we can sit down and talk about it." The creamy dish, adapted from a recipe passed down from her Great-aunt Toddie, signifies so much for Wynonna.

She says casseroles were a staple when she was growing up in Ashland, Kentucky, because her family was poor, and those dishes went a long way. Wynonna remembers both of her grandmothers being excellent cooks and saw what amazing things they could accomplish with whatever they had. "Watching them cook was like magic for me," she recalls. "Whatever they made came from love. What they could bring out of the kitchen was a miracle."

"When I buy the ingredients to make that favorite broccoli-rice casserole, it's a memory that goes back 49 years for me," Wynonna adds. "It's not just a casserole. It is what draws my daughter to me in the kitchen. You know, the most difficult relationship is the one between a daughter and mother," she says, speaking from a life of experience.

The world met Wynonna when she began performing with her mother, Naomi, in the early 1980s as The Judds. With Wynonna singing lead and playing guitar and Naomi singing backup, the duo stormed country music for almost 10 years. They won multiple awards and sold more than 20 million albums. Unfortunately, Naomi's diagnosis of hepatitis C spelled the end of The Judds, except for rare appearances. Wynonna, however, began to perform solo—earning more awards and selling more than 10 million albums.

Though she's often on the road, when she's home, Wynonna enforces at least one rule. She, Grace, her 20-year-old son, Elijah, and her musician husband Cactus Moser eat meals together. "I force the kids to have conversations," she says. "For me, the supper table is important for fellowship."

This belief comes straight from her mother. No matter what success or failure a family member has experienced, each person gets a chance to talk. "Through good and bad times and disappointments, we were in a state of bliss and appreciation for what we would receive. Food was always what bound us in that moment," says Wynonna. With a family full of strong personalities, they often disagree about everything—but the table is the place where everyone comes together.

albums & awards

After her mother's illness, Wynonna began to perform solo.

In the 10 years The Judds dominated the country music scene, they sold more than 20 million records and won more than 60 industry awards.

In 1994, the Academy of Country Music named Wynonna the Top Female Vocalist of the Year.

Wynonna has won five Grammy Awards.

Wynonna's 1992 self-titled solo album went quintuple platinum.

"WATCHING THEM COOK WAS LIKE MAGIC FOR ME... WHATEVER THEY MADE CAME FROM LOVE," WYNONNA SAYS OF HER GRANDMOTHERS.

GRACE'S FAVORITE BROCCOLI-RICE CASSEROLE

makes: 8 to 10 servings   **hands-on time: 20 min.**
total time: 40 min.

When Wynonna's teenage daughter, Grace, needs a little extra TLC, she asks for this comforting casserole, which is adapted from a favorite recipe handed down by Wynonna's Great-aunt Toddie.

1	(16-oz.) pkg. frozen broccoli florets or spears
1	lb. processed cheese, cubed
1	(10¾-oz.) can cream of chicken soup
1	cup cooked white rice
1	cup cooked brown rice
½	cup milk
1	Tbsp. Worcestershire sauce
	Table salt
	Freshly ground black pepper
1	(6-oz.) can French fried onions

1. Preheat oven to 350°. Prepare broccoli according to package directions. Stir together broccoli and next 6 ingredients in a large bowl. Add salt and pepper to taste. Spoon broccoli mixture into a lightly greased 11- x 7-inch baking dish. Top with French fried onions.

2. Bake at 350° for 20 to 25 minutes or until golden and bubbly.

NOTE: We tested with Velveeta Original Pasteurized Prepared Cheese Product and French's Original French Fried Onions.

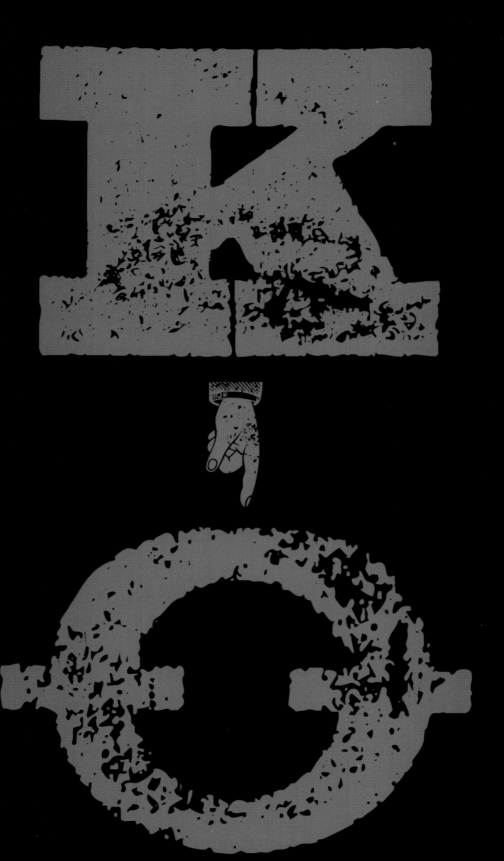

Jana Kramer

Jana Kramer began her professional career as an actress, best known as Alex Dupre on the show *One Tree Hill*. But these days, you'll hear her singing country songs, inspired by legendary voices from the past.

As a little girl, Jana Kramer fell in love with country music in her Grandma Marge's kitchen. "We loved to bake cookies together while we listened to Patsy Cline, Loretta Lynn, and June Carter," recalls the singer and actress. Jana wore an apron, just like her grandmother, and learned the words to those songs. She also learned about baking from Grandma Marge, the cooking guru in the family, as well as the lesson that straying from the recipe can often lead to good things. "She knows just what to add or subtract."

Grandma Marge taught Jana how to make pies and other sweets, and Jana's Chocolate Chip Cookies are still some of her favorites, particularly because they include a grated chocolate bar. "They just remind me of grandma," she says.

Before making a splash on the country music scene, the slender brunette lived in Los Angeles for about 10 years working as a successful actress, with memorable roles on the television shows *Friday Night Lights* and *One Tree Hill*. In 2011, she took a break from acting and stepped into country music—a passion that had begun in her grandmother's kitchen. "Acting gave me the guts to follow my heart to pursue my music," Jana explains.

She got a record deal, recorded an album, began touring, and has since played with big-time acts such as Brad Paisley and Blake Shelton. "Country

albums & awards

Jana Kramer's 2012 self-titled debut album reached number 5 on the country charts, and "Why Ya Wanna," a single from it, was certified gold.

In 2013, Jana won the American Country Music Award for Top New Female Vocalist.

Jana Kramer began her professional career as an actress, with notable roles on the television series *Friday Night Lights* and *One Tree Hill*.

music is in my blood," she says. "I love country music because it tells a story, and I have a lot of stories to tell. I love acting, but my heart and soul is in singing."

You can hear that soul in her voice when she sings moving songs such as "Why Ya Wanna," the story of a woman whose love is rekindled the minute an old flame appears. Jana's sound is distinctly country—even Southern, with a hint of twang—which might be a bit of a surprise considering she grew up in Rochester, Michigan, just north of Detroit.

Jana's family food traditions have been strong her entire life, especially in the summer. She spent a lot of time with her Grandma Marge in the small town of Gaylord, in the northern part of her home state. There is a lake there, and each year, all of Jana's aunts, uncles, cousins, and grandparents gather for the Fourth of July week. Every night has a different theme—Mexican on Mondays, seafood on Tuesdays, etc.—and all of them, including the kids, take turns cooking meals. "When I was younger, the best I could do was make macaroni and cheese for everybody," recalls Jana. Now that she's an adult, she serves Beef Burritos for the whole family one night of the week.

The family takes the whole "theme night" idea a step further. "To make it cheesier, we even dress up," Jana adds. "Imagine the whole clan in sombreros taking whacks at a piñata!"

BEEF BURRITOS

**makes: 6 to 8 servings   hands-on time: 35 min.
total time: 1 hour, 25 min.**

**These simply
fresh and delicious
burritos make a
wonderful hot
lunch or dinner.**

1 lb. lean ground beef
1 (6-oz.) can refried beans
1 cup mild or hot salsa
1 (15-oz.) can chili without beans
1 (4-oz.) can chopped green chiles, drained
1 (10¾-oz.) can Cheddar cheese soup

10 (8-inch) flour tortillas
2 cups (8 oz.) shredded Cheddar cheese

Toppings: chopped tomatoes, sliced green onions, sliced black olives, chopped lettuce, sour cream, guacamole, additional salsa

1. Preheat oven to 350°. Brown ground beef in a large skillet over medium-high heat, stirring often, 6 to 8 minutes or until meat crumbles and is no longer pink; drain. Stir in refried beans.

2. Cook salsa, chili, green chiles, and soup in a medium saucepan over low heat, stirring occasionally, 3 to 5 minutes or until heated through. Remove from heat.

3. Stir ½ cup of salsa mixture into beef mixture. Pour 1 cup of salsa mixture into a lightly greased 13- x 9-inch baking dish. Set aside remaining salsa mixture.

4. Spoon about ¼ cup of beef mixture evenly down center of each tortilla. Sprinkle 1 to 2 Tbsp. shredded cheese over beef mixture, and roll up. Arrange rolled tortillas, seam side down, in baking dish. Pour remaining salsa mixture over tortillas, and sprinkle with remaining cheese.

5. Bake at 350° for 30 to 40 minutes or until bubbly. Let stand 10 minutes. Serve with desired toppings.

JANA RECALLS LEARNING TO COOK IN HER GRANDMA'S KITCHEN. ❝WE LOVED TO BAKE COOKIES TOGETHER WHILE WE LISTENED TO PATSY CLINE, LORETTA LYNN, AND JUNE CARTER.❞

JANA'S CHOCOLATE CHIP COOKIES

makes: about 4½ dozen   **hands-on time: 45 min.**
total time: 2 hours, 5 min.

Parchment paper
2¼ cups uncooked regular oats
2 cups all-purpose flour
1 tsp. baking powder
1 tsp. baking soda
½ tsp. table salt
1 cup unsalted butter, softened
1 cup granulated sugar
1 cup firmly packed light brown sugar
2 large eggs
1 tsp. vanilla extract
1 (12-oz.) package semisweet chocolate chips
1 (4.4-oz.) milk chocolate bar, grated
1½ cups chopped pecans

1. Line baking sheets with parchment paper; preheat oven to 375°. Pulse oats in food processor until powdery. Whisk together oats, flour, and next 3 ingredients in a large bowl; set aside.

2. Beat butter and sugars at medium speed with an electric mixer until fluffy. Add eggs, one at time, beating until blended. Stir in vanilla extract.

3. Gradually add flour mixture, beating at low speed until blended. Stir in chocolate chips, grated chocolate bar, and nuts.

4. Using a 1½-inch scoop, drop dough 2 inches apart onto parchment paper-lined baking sheets. Bake at 375° for 8 to 10 minutes.

5. Cool cookies 2 to 3 minutes on baking sheets. Transfer cookies to wire racks; cool completely.

★ ★ ★

Ground oats and chopped pecans give these chewy cookies nice texture, and a grated milk chocolate bar gives the chocolate chips a boost.

★ ★ ★

Miranda Lambert

Miranda Lambert hit the country music scene after successfully competing on the show *Nashville Star* more than a decade ago. In the years since, she has become one of the industry's most recognizable, feisty, and soulful performers.

If your parents are both private investigators, it's hard to make mischief. That was what it was like for singer Miranda Lambert when she was a child. In fact, it was impossible. "I could never get anything past them," she says of her mom and dad. "I usually tell people that my mom knew what I was doing before I did it. I think both my parents were pretty rowdy growing up, so they were on to everything I could think of sneaking past them."

Rick and Beverly Lambert were mostly tracking cheating spouses in the small town of Lindale, Texas, a place where, Miranda says, gossip usually beat you home. But that business wasn't always great, and when the family struggled financially, Rick took it on himself to provide food right from the land by starting a subsistence farm.

"We didn't go to the store for anything but milk," Miranda says. Her mother made bread and canned what she could from the garden. They raised chickens, pigs, and rabbits. "We literally lived off the land."

Beverly, who is a great cook, took what they had, sat Miranda on a stool by the kitchen counter, and taught her how to prepare it. "One thing my mom always insisted on is that our family eat dinner together every night," says Miranda. "That was her way of making everyone chip in to make it happen."

Mexican food was a staple in the Lambert house, and Beverly became known for her enchiladas. Miranda never quite mastered the techniques for Mexican dishes, but she learned how to make her Mama's Meatloaf (the secret ingredient: breakfast sausage). It's a favorite comfort food served each year on Miranda's birthday.

Through it all, Miranda was singing, sometimes country duets with her dad and, when she was in her late teens, feisty, soulful songs in honky-tonks around Texas. She has a fiery demeanor on stage, a style that translated well when she competed on the show *Nashville Star* in 2003. Miranda finished third, which earned her a record deal with Sony Nashville.

A few years later, she met her would-be husband, Blake Shelton, while they performed the duet "You're the Reason God Made Oklahoma" on a CMT special. (Interestingly, she had grown up singing that song with her dad.) They were both immediately smitten. "There was definitely chemistry," she says.

The couple married in 2011 and now live in Tishomingo, Oklahoma, where they are developing their own family food traditions. Apparently, Blake is a big fan of appetizers, so Miranda often makes stuffed jalapeños. But his favorite dish of hers is a simple corn casserole, a nod to the comfort foods they both crave when they're home together.

❧ albums & awards ❧

In 2003, the singer-songwriter came in third in the television competition *Nashville Star*.

In 2011, Miranda Lambert formed an all-girl singing group, the Pistol Annies.

Miranda has been honored multiple times by the major music organizations, including CMT Music Awards, Grammy Awards, Academy of Country Music Awards, and Country Music Association Awards.

Miranda's second album, *Crazy Ex-Girlfriend,* was released in 2007.

"MY MAMA'S MEATLOAF HAS ALWAYS BEEN MY FAVORITE RECIPE. IT'S BEEN THE CHOICE 'BIRTHDAY DISH' FOR ME AND MY BROTHER SINCE WE WERE LITTLE."

This down-home dish, perfected by Miranda Lambert's mother, Beverly Lambert, features pork sausage, ground beef, and a sweet ketchup-based topping.

MAMA'S MEATLOAF

makes: 10 servings   hands-on time: 25 min.   total time: 2 hours

2	lb. lean ground beef		1	Tbsp. Worcestershire sauce
1	lb. ground pork sausage		1	tsp. yellow mustard
18	saltine crackers, crushed		½	cup firmly packed brown sugar, divided
½	green bell pepper, diced		½	cup ketchup
½	onion, finely chopped			
2	large eggs, lightly beaten			

1. Preheat oven to 350°. Combine first 8 ingredients and ¼ cup brown sugar in a medium bowl just until blended. Place mixture in a lightly greased 11- x 7-inch baking dish, and shape mixture into a 10- x 5-inch loaf.

2. Bake at 350° for 1 hour. Remove from oven, and drain. Stir together ketchup and remaining ¼ cup brown sugar; pour over meatloaf. Bake 15 more minutes or until a meat thermometer inserted into thickest portion registers 160°. Remove from oven; let stand 20 minutes. Remove from baking dish before slicing.

TIP

For a perfectly moist meatloaf, make sure to blend the mixture until everything is just incorporated.

Out of Summertime ✍ I LOVE YOU THIS BIG ✍ CLEAR A
DAY ★ The Trouble with Girls ♫ WATER TOWER TOWN ♫
WALK IN THE COUNTRY ★ ★ ★ Better Than Th
✍ WRITE MY NUMBER ON YOUR HAND ✍ DIRTY DISHES
★ ★ You Make That Look Good ★ BACK ON THE GROUND ★
♫ THAT OLD KING JAMES ♫ Now ★ ★

★ ★ SEE YOU TONIGHT ★ ★ ★ GET GONE WITH YOU ♫
Feelin' It ✍ FEEL GOOD SUMMER SONG ✍ BUZZIN'
Can You Feel It ★ ★ THE DASH ★ ★ BLUE JEAN BAB
Forget To Forget You ♫ I DON'T WANNA BE YOUR FRIEND ♫
✍ CAROLINA MOON ✍ Something More
★ ROLL YOUR WINDOW DOWN ★ ★ ★ BEFORE MIDNIGHT ★

Scotty McCreery

This young man's surprisingly seasoned voice earned him fame as the first country music winner on American Idol. Although Scotty McCreery is a great singer, he admits he's not a good cook— but he's got grandmothers and great-grandmothers who were.

Scotty McCreery says everybody in his hometown of Garner, North Carolina, is pretty much well acquainted with everyone else. "It's the kind of place where when you go grocery shopping, you run into your neighbors," adds the 20-year-old singer-songwriter, who has arguably become the biggest thing to ever come out of that small town.

Scotty grew up singing in church and was part of a choral group in high school. He was just a regular kid. He pitched on the high-school baseball team. He worked side jobs at both an auto mechanic shop and a grocery store. At the age of 17, Scotty auditioned and landed a spot on the television competition series *American Idol*. He was an instant hit, mainly because such an unexpected voice—a deep and soulful baritone—was coming from such a baby-faced, bright-eyed young man. (Close your eyes when you listen to Scotty sing, and you'll swear you're hearing a classic country crooner approaching midlife.)

He went on to become the show's youngest winner, as well as its first in the country music genre. After the competition, Scotty's debut album was certified platinum and included two top 20 hits. He has since made a Christmas album, released his third album, and continues to tour across the country singing and playing guitar.

When he's home, Scotty doesn't do much cooking himself—"It's never been something I've taken a liking to." But he does come from a long line of fine cooks, beginning with his Great-grandma Lillian, who was best known for her sweets. Her Pound Cake became one of the most popular recipes at family functions, and Scotty was a fan.

Another familiar family sweet is his Grandma Paquita's Spanish Flan. Scotty's grandmother is Puerto Rican, and his father was born in San Juan before the family moved to the States. "The flan is her specialty," says Scotty. "My dad grew up with it, and the family loves it for sure." The singer admits that it's not quite his favorite dessert—he says its otherworldly texture is an acquired taste.

On the savory side, Scotty believes that his maternal grandmother, Janet Cooke, could have made up her recipe for Broccoli Cornbread as a whimsical way to get the grandkids to eat their green vegetables. "She's a ball of fun," he says. "She always has a big smile on her face, and anytime she sees her grandchildren, she's running after them."

And even though Scotty never met his Great-grandmother Cookie Cooke, her Brunswick Stew remains a family tradition. The story is that Cookie made the stew in a huge pot, using everything she could find in her garden and around her house—all the vegetables and even the chicken.

albums & awards

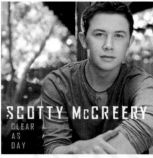

His debut album was certified platinum and included two top 20 hits.

In 2011, Scotty McCreery won the American Country Award for New Artist of the Year.

He won the Academy of Country Music Award for Best New Artist in 2012.

Scotty won the CMT Award *USA Weekend* Breakthrough Video of the Year for "The Trouble with Girls" in 2012.

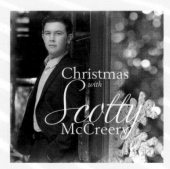

Scotty grew up singing at church and in school. His big break came when he won the 10th season of *American Idol*.

SCOTTY COMES FROM A LONG LINE OF FINE COOKS, LIKE HIS GREAT-GRANDMA LILLIAN, WHOSE SPECIALTY WAS BAKED SWEETS.

This recipe is at least four generations old, having been handed down on Scotty's mom's side of the family. It's extra good with a dollop of whipped cream and fresh blueberries.

GREAT-GRANDMA LILLIAN'S POUND CAKE

makes: 10 to 12 servings   hands-on time: 35 min.
total time: 2 hours, 30 min.

1 cup butter	3 cups all-purpose flour
½ cup shortening	1 tsp. baking powder
3 cups sugar	⅓ tsp. table salt
6 large eggs	1 cup milk
1 Tbsp. vanilla extract	

1. Preheat oven to 350°. Beat butter, shortening, and sugar at medium speed with an electric mixer 2 minutes or until light and fluffy.

2. Add eggs, and beat 1 minute until creamy. Beat in vanilla just until blended.

3. Combine flour, baking powder, and salt; add to butter mixture alternately with milk, beginning and ending with flour mixture. Beat 5 minutes.

4. Spoon batter into a greased and floured 10-inch tube pan.* Bake at 350° for 1 hour to 1 hour and 10 minutes or until a long wooden pick inserted in center of cake comes out clean. Cool in pan on a wire rack 10 to 15 minutes; remove from pan to wire rack, and cool completely (about 1 hour and 25 minutes).

*If you prefer pound cake squares, use a 13- x 9-inch baking pan. Bake 50 to 55 minutes; cool as directed, and cut into 12 squares.

SCOTTY MCCREERY

❝ THE FLAN IS HER SPECIALTY. MY DAD GREW UP WITH IT, AND THE FAMILY LOVES IT FOR SURE. ❞

GRANDMA PAQUITA'S SPANISH FLAN

**makes: 8 servings   hands-on time: 20 min., including chilling
total time: 10 hours, 50 min.**

1	cup sugar, divided
3	large eggs
2	(12-oz.) cans evaporated milk
¼	tsp. table salt
¼	tsp. vanilla extract

1. Preheat oven to 325°. Cook ½ cup sugar in a 10-inch nonstick skillet over medium heat about 2 minutes, shaking skillet until sugar melts and is light golden brown.

2. Quickly and carefully pour hot caramelized sugar into a 9-inch round cake pan with 2-inch sides. Using oven mitts, tilt cake pan to evenly coat bottom and seal edges.

3. Process eggs, milk, salt, vanilla, and remaining sugar in a blender until smooth. Pour mixture over caramelized sugar in cake pan. Cover cake pan with aluminum foil; place in a large shallow pan. Add hot tap water (about 115°) halfway up sides of cake pan.

4. Bake at 325° for 1½ hours or just until a knife inserted into the center comes out clean. Remove pan from oven; remove cake pan from water, and place on a wire rack. Uncover cake pan, and cool completely (about 1 hour). Cover and chill at least 8 hours.

5. Run a knife around edges to loosen, and invert onto a serving plate. Cut into wedges to serve.

★ ★ ★

Scotty McCreery's Grandmother Paquita is a native of Puerto Rico, and his dad was born there. Her sweet, velvety treat is one of his dad's favorite desserts.

★ ★ ★

GRANDMA JANET'S BROCCOLI CORNBREAD

makes: 8 to 10 servings   **hands-on time: 25 min.**
total time: 55 min.

★ ★ ★

This mildly sweet and delicious cornbread—a decidedly great way to get your broccoli—comes from Scotty's maternal grandmother, Janet Cooke.

★ ★ ★

1	(10-oz.) pkg. frozen, chopped broccoli
1	medium onion, chopped
½	cup butter or margarine, melted
3	large eggs, lightly beaten
1	cup small-curd cottage cheese
1	tsp. table salt
1	(8.5-oz.) package corn muffin mix

1. Preheat oven to 400°. Prepare broccoli according to package directions; drain well, and set aside. Cook onion in butter in medium skillet over medium heat 4 to 5 minutes or until softened. Remove from heat; set aside.

2. Combine eggs, cottage cheese, and salt in a large bowl. Add corn muffin mix, cooked onions, and broccoli; stir just until blended.

3. Pour batter into a lightly greased 9-inch square baking pan.

4. Bake at 400° for 20 to 25 minutes or until light golden brown. Remove cornbread from pan; serve immediately.

NOTE: We tested with Jiffy Corn Muffin Mix.

ACCORDING TO SCOTTY'S MOTHER, JUDY, **THIS RECIPE ORIGINATED WITH HIS GREAT-GRANDMOTHER COOKIE COOKE,** WHO WAS BORN IN 1898.

GREAT-GRANDMA COOKIE COOKE'S BRUNSWICK STEW

makes: 8 to 10 servings (12 cups)   **hands-on time: 45 min.**
total time: 2 hours, 50 min.

1   lb. ground beef
1   small onion, chopped
3   cups chicken broth
2   cups fresh or frozen lima beans, thawed
2   cups fresh or frozen corn, thawed
1   large russet potato, peeled and cubed
2   (14½-oz.) cans diced tomatoes, undrained
3   Tbsp. butter
3½ cups chopped rotisserie chicken
4   cups chopped green cabbage, cooked
¼   tsp. ground red pepper
1   tsp. freshly ground black pepper
Table salt to taste
Hot sauce to taste

1. Cook ground beef and onion in a large Dutch oven over medium heat 6 to 8 minutes or until meat crumbles and is no longer pink. Drain meat mixture; return to Dutch oven.

2. Add chicken broth and next 9 ingredients. Bring mixture to a boil over medium-high heat; reduce heat to medium-low, and simmer at least 2 hours. Season to taste with salt and hot sauce.

★ ★ ★

Considering the many hearty ingredients used, it's no surprise that the longer this stew cooks, the better it gets!

★ ★ ★

Craig Morgan

Singer-songwriter Craig Morgan lives life to the extreme. Despite his reality show—which documents numerous outdoor exploits—and long tours, Craig carves out a generous amount of peaceful time with his family. Peaceful, that is, until he breaks out his bagpipes!

One of Craig Morgan's favorite stories begins with a one-eyed guide in the wild terrain of Alaska. They were on the lookout for grizzlies, when a bear came within 100 yards, just on the other side of a creek. The guide warned him to shoot before the grizzly crossed the water. "But I wanted to get closer. I'm a man, and I've got a mustache," Craig says with a laugh. He possesses an insatiable desire for adrenaline rushes, as evidenced by his reality show *Craig Morgan: All Access Outdoors*, where one week he's surfing in Hawaii, and the next he's exploring the backcountry of Alaska with a half-blind local and a photographer from the show to record it.

As Craig's story begins to wind up, he gets more and more excited. "I got close enough, and I shot him—but he didn't fall!" The bear started running and got within 45 yards. "He was staring dead at me," recalls Craig, "but I wasn't worried because I knew I could outrun the guide and the cameraman!" Thankfully, he did eventually fell the grizzly, and the three men made it out safely with one heckuva story.

From a young age, hunting has been a big part of Craig's life. He and his three siblings grew up in Kingston Springs, Tennessee, southwest of Nashville, where his dad was a working musician, a bass player. "We were lower middle class," Craig says. "Wild game was important to us. Our garden was important to us. We had to develop the skills to harvest." He marvels at how they got by, "My mom was the best. I don't know how she did it," he says. "You'd look in the cupboard and just see two things. And she'd end up making a four-course meal."

"I've always felt that I've been very blessed," says Craig. "There's someone much more important than me in charge of this, because if you look at where I came from and the things that had to happen for me to be here, there is absolutely no way anyone could have planned this."

His father had six brothers, and all of Craig's uncles had four kids each. (You get four guesses about how many children Craig and his wife, Karen, have.) So Fourth of July family reunions were a really big deal. "We'd start on the whole hogs the night before," Craig recalls, "and there were always fresh vegetables from my granddad's garden." His grandfather Poppy was known for his homemade vinegar-based barbecue sauce, which makes for a perfect companion to pulled pork.

Despite his dad's career in the Nashville scene and the fact that music came naturally to him, Craig never imagined he would follow that path. "At first I thought music was going to be a full-time hobby," he explains. "I grew up going, 'The last thing I'm going to do is this.'"

So he bounced a bit from job to job—working as everything from an EMT to a contractor, sheriff's deputy, and grocery store dairy manager. He also served nearly 20 years in the U.S. military, with 10 years of active duty and another nine in the reserves.

Craig's mentality was to work a lot, play a little music. Unexpectedly, his songs—narrative-driven lyrics told with a sound that blends traditional country with a little Southern rock—began to take hold, and he landed a record deal in 2000. He was in his mid-thirties, and he had no more need to bounce. Eight years later, Craig stepped onstage to accept his induction into the Grand Ole Opry. "It wasn't until the Opry membership that I knew it was going to be my full-time job," he adds.

"I've always felt that I've been very blessed," says Craig. "There's someone much more important than me in charge of this, because if you look at where I

(continued on page 194)

CRAIG HAS MAINTAINED **A STRONG CONNECTION TO THE LAND.** HE AND KAREN KEEP BEES AND CHICKENS AND MANAGE A HUGE VEGETABLE GARDEN ON THEIR FARM.

I FEEL LIKE I JUST GOT STARTED. I FEEL LIKE I'M 25 YEARS OLD AND SAYING, 'WOW, I HOPE I MAKE IT IN THE MUSIC BUSINESS.'

came from and the things that had to happen for me to be here, there is absolutely no way anyone could have planned this."

To date, Craig has scored 14 Top 10 hits, but if you ask him what music he's working on, he'll likely tell you about the bagpipes he's teaching himself to play. Lucky for his family and neighbors, the Morgans have plenty of land on their farm in Dickson, Tennessee.

Craig has maintained a strong connection to the land. He and Karen keep bees and chickens and manage a huge vegetable garden on their farm.

"Every vegetable in the house is either home-grown or organic," Craig notes. "We know where it's coming from. We cook anything and love mixing up flavors. We get excited when we can make things

like salsa from our own garden."

Sourcing is important to Craig, even when he's hunting wild game with bows or guns. For more than 10 years, he has hunted elk in Utah, Montana, and Wyoming, and he says he gets at least one each hunting season for their freezer. "I've hunted more than I've been successful," he admits. "The good thing is that you know what you're getting."

Elk became the main ingredient for one of his favorite recipes, Elk Shepherd's Pie. Craig actually helped chef and close friend Victor Lugo develop the recipe. Victor owns Lugo's, a small, white-tablecloth restaurant right downtown on Main Street in Dickson.

"Victor and I share the same passion for organic, fresh food, and self-sustainment," explains Craig.

From a young age, hunting has been a big part of Craig's life.

The consummate performer, Craig strives to keep his live shows special. In fact, he's been known to break out the bagpipes on occasion to great applause.

"I introduced him to elk and venison, and he was like a kid in a candy store."

Craig's passion for healthy food has had an influence on his band, too. While touring, the guys have developed an interest in organic vegetables, and no one complains when Craig does a little bit of cooking. "Every turkey season, I'll take a bird and grill it for the band. We've had a few vegetarians," he jokes, "but they don't last long."

～ albums & awards ～

Nominated for Radio Music Award
category Song of the Year/Country Radio for
"That's What I Love About Sunday," 2005

Nominated for ICM Award
category Song of the Year for
"That's What I Love About Sunday," 2005

Won ICM Award category Video of the Year for
"That's What I Love About Sunday," 2005

Won ICM Award category
Mainstream Country Artist, 2005

Nominated for Academy of Country Music Award
category Top New Male Vocalist, 2006

Nominated for Academy of Country Music Award
category Top New Male Vocalist, 2007

Craig released his sixth album, *This Ole Boy*, in 2012.

The Journey (Livin' Hits) is Craig's latest album.

"VICTOR LUGO AND I SHARE THE SAME PASSION FOR ORGANIC, FRESH FOOD AND SELF-SUSTAINMENT. I INTRODUCED HIM TO ELK AND VENISON, AND **HE WAS LIKE A KID IN A CANDY STORE.**"

ELK SHEPHERD'S PIE

makes: 8 servings   **hands-on time: 50 min.**
total time: 2 hours, 50 min.

3	lbs. cubed elk stew meat*
1½	Tbsp. canola oil
2	cups dry red wine
4	cups beef broth, divided
8	medium-size baking potatoes, peeled and cubed
3	tsp. table salt, divided
½	tsp. freshly ground black pepper

¾	cup unsalted butter, divided
¾	tsp. granulated garlic
⅔	cup heavy cream
1	cup all-purpose flour
1	(16-oz.) package frozen peas and diced carrots, thawed
1	(14-oz.) package frozen diced carrots, onion and celery, thawed

1. Cook meat, in 3 batches, in 1½ Tbsp. hot oil in a large Dutch oven over medium-high heat 4 to 5 minutes or until browned on all sides. Set aside, and keep warm.

2. Add red wine to Dutch oven, and cook 2 minutes, stirring to loosen browned bits from bottom of pan. Return meat to pan, and add 2½ cups beef broth. Bring meat mixture to a boil; cover, reduce heat to medium-low, and simmer 1½ hours.

3. Remove lid from Dutch oven; increase heat to medium-high, and bring meat mixture to a boil. Cook, stirring occasionally, 40 to 45 minutes or until liquid reduces to about ¼ cup.

4. Bring potatoes, 2 tsp. salt, and water to cover to a boil in another large Dutch oven, and cook 10 minutes or until potatoes are tender. Drain potatoes, and return to Dutch oven. Mash potatoes with 1 tsp. salt, ½ tsp. pepper, ½ cup butter, and garlic. Stir in cream; set aside, and keep warm.

5. Preheat oven to 400°. Sprinkle flour over meat mixture in Dutch oven, and cook, stirring, until smooth. Stir in vegetables and remaining beef broth. Spoon meat mixture into a lightly greased 13- x 9-inch baking dish. Spread mashed potatoes over meat, leaving a 1-inch margin around potatoes.

6. Melt remaining ¼ cup butter; brush over potatoes. Bake at 400° for 25 minutes or until bubbly; increase oven temperature to broil, and broil 5 to 7 minutes or until golden brown.

*Venison, bison, or lean beef may be substituted if elk is unavailable.

★ ★ ★

Craig Morgan and his wife, Karen, served this at a wild game dinner they hosted. Craig, an avid hunter, harvested the elk himself, and both he and Karen are organic gardeners who love to cook at home. They worked with their friend chef Victor Lugo (shown at left on opposite page), who owns a restaurant in Dickson, Tennessee, close to where the Morgans live, to put on the dinner.

★ ★ ★

The Oak Ridge Boys

Legendary country stars The Oak Ridge Boys have spent the last four decades performing all over the world. As you might imagine, they've become as close as brothers, and a lot of that bonding has happened over food.

One tradition The Oak Ridge Boys still honor, even after more than 40 years of performing together, is gathering in a nice restaurant for a big meal after a show. "It's one of our great pleasures," says lead singer Duane Allen. "We can put our feet up and eat something good." The legendary quartet still shares its four-part harmonies when performing 150 shows a year. Despite their varied backgrounds, the four men remain tight.

"If you want to know how country boys lived, you can talk to me," says Duane, who grew up on a cotton and corn farm in Taylor Town, Texas. Duane was the baby of six children, and his mother kept all those mouths fed with huge lunches involving three meats, six or seven vegetables, and at least three pies. These days, at their home in Hendersonville, Tennessee, Duane and his wife, Norah, enjoy simpler spreads, including quick dishes like Fresh Fruit Salad and Norah's mother's Cheesy Potato Soup with Almonds.

Joe Bonsall, the quartet's tenor, had anything but a farm life, having grown up in Philadelphia. His mother was from North Carolina. "She could make the best fried chicken," Joe recalls. He enjoyed ethnic foods, such as pierogies and pretzels from his Polish friends. One of his favorite things was rice pudding with a scoop or two of chocolate ice cream. Years later, he mentioned that childhood treat to his wife,

Mary, and she whipped out her own Old-Fashioned Rice Pudding recipe. "I swear it is the best I have ever had," he says.

Richard Sterban, the group's bass singer, grew up near Philadelphia in Camden, New Jersey. His mother's side of the family was Italian, and he says he could eat pasta nearly every day of the year. At Thanksgiving his family always had rigatoni and meatballs before the turkey and other trimmings. "I was taught that you've gotta have the pasta first!" he says. Perhaps that's why one of his favorite recipes is the Seafood Pasta Sauce his wife, Donna, makes.

Baritone singer and Alabama native William Lee Golden was raised on a farm where his father grew cotton, peanuts, soybeans, and wheat. It was peaceful, with plenty of room to run wild and clear views of beautiful sunsets. William Lee says peanut butter is one of his essential comfort foods, always reminding him of his dad's crops. His mother was a wonderful cook, especially skilled at making sweets. His sister, Lanette, inherited that talent and once brought an incredible Orange Dreamsicle Cake to a family gathering. "It was absolutely such a delight that we had to have the recipe," says William Lee. "It's become our new favorite." His wife, Brenda, often prepares that dessert for guests at their home in Hendersonville, Tennessee, a 1786 estate nicknamed Golden Era Plantation.

❧ albums & awards ❧

The Oak Ridge Boys' biggest hit "Elvira" was featured on their 1981 release *Fancy Free*.

To date, The Oak Ridge Boys have sold more than 30 million records and have had more than a dozen national number one hits and 30 Top 10 singles.

They've won multiple Grammys, Academy of Country Music, and Country Music Association Awards.

The song "Bobbie Sue" reached number twelve on the Hot 100 singles chart in 1982.

"IF YOU WANT TO KNOW HOW COUNTRY BOYS LIVED, YOU CAN TALK TO ME," SAYS DUANE ABOUT THE HUGE FAMILY SPREADS HIS MOTHER PREPARED FOR HER SIX CHILDREN.

Duane Allen likes to eat more simply than when he was young. He makes this as a quick dessert and serves it with pound cake or brownies.

FRESH FRUIT SALAD

makes: 6 servings (about 6½ cups)   hands-on time: 20 min.
total time: 20 min.

2	large oranges	2	small bananas, sliced
2	large red delicious apples		(about 1 cup)
1	cup chopped fresh pineapple	½	cup toasted chopped pecans
1	cup seedless grapes, halved		Garnish: fresh mint leaves

1. Peel, section, and chop oranges, reserving juice. Place oranges and juice in a large bowl. Cut apples into ³/₄-inch cubes, and add to oranges and juice. Add pineapple and grapes, and toss gently. Cover and chill.

2. Add bananas and pecans, and toss gently.

TIP

Cutting fresh pineapple can be a chore.
To simplify the process, remove the "eyes," which grow
in diagonal lines on the pineapple in strips.

CHEESY POTATO SOUP WITH ALMONDS

makes: 4 servings (6 cups)   **hands-on time: 15 min.**
total time: 35 min.

3   large baking potatoes,
    peeled and diced
1   tsp. table salt
½   (16-oz.) box 2% pasteurized
    cheese product
1   Tbsp. butter

Table salt to taste
Freshly ground black pepper
    to taste
½   cup toasted sliced almonds
Garnish: chopped fresh chives

1. Bring potatoes, 1 tsp. salt, and 4 cups water to a boil in a large saucepan over medium-high heat. Cook 10 minutes or until potatoes are tender. Do not drain.

2. Cut cheese into ½-inch cubes. Add cheese and butter to potato mixture, stirring until cheese melts. Add salt and pepper to taste.

3. Top each serving with sliced almonds.

This recipe came from Duane Allen's mother-in-law. It's not difficult to throw together. Serve it with hot, homemade cornbread (made in a cast-iron skillet, of course) and a fresh garden salad.

TIP

Other accompaniments to this tasty soup might include hushpuppies, slaw, and a fresh fruit salad.

JOE BONSALL SAYS HIS WIFE, MARY, SERVES HER RICE PUDDING LIKE HE REMEMBERS HAVING IT IN DINERS IN PHILLY: "WARM WITH ICE CREAM, VANILLA FOR HER AND CHOCOLATE FOR ME."

★ ★ ★

Mary sometimes uses dried cherries instead of the raisins, which, in Joe's opinion, make it even more delicious.

★ ★ ★

MARY'S OLD-FASHIONED RICE PUDDING

**makes: 6 servings   hands-on time: 15 min.
total time: 1 hour, 15 min.**

3½ cups soy milk
½   cup uncooked jasmine rice
⅓   cup sugar
½   tsp. table salt
½   cup raisins or dried cherries

1   tsp. vanilla extract
Ground cinnamon (optional)
Vanilla or chocolate ice cream
     (optional)

1. Preheat oven to 325°. Combine milk and next 3 ingredients in a large saucepan. Bring to a boil over medium heat, stirring constantly.

2. Pour rice mixture into a lightly greased 1½-qt. baking dish. Cover and bake at 325° for 20 minutes. Stir rice mixture; cover and bake for 20 more minutes.

3. Stir raisins and vanilla into rice mixture; cover and bake for 20 more minutes.

4. Remove from oven to a wire rack, and cool 15 minutes. Sprinkle with cinnamon, if desired. Serve warm or chilled with ice cream, if desired.

THE OAK RIDGE BOYS

"I WAS TAUGHT THAT YOU GOTTA HAVE THE PASTA FIRST!" SAYS RICHARD STERBAN.

DONNA'S SEAFOOD PASTA SAUCE

makes: 8 servings (8 cups sauce)   **hands-on time: 35 min.**
total time: 2 hours, 15 min.

2   Tbsp. minced garlic
2   Tbsp. olive oil
2   (26.46-oz.) boxes strained tomatoes
1   (26.46-oz.) box diced tomatoes
2   tsp. herbs de Provence
2   tsp. dried oregano
1   tsp. crushed red pepper flakes (optional)
Table salt to taste
Freshly ground black pepper to taste

1   (16-oz.) package angel hair pasta
24   fresh mussels, washed, shells scrubbed and debearded
24   fresh clams in shells, scrubbed
1   lb. large (21-25 count) shrimp, peeled and deveined
Italian bread
Garnish: fresh parsley leaves

★ ★ ★

Richard's Alabama-born wife, Donna, developed this recipe after eating pasta with her Italian New Jersey in-laws.

★ ★ ★

1. Cook garlic in hot oil over medium-high heat in a large Dutch oven, stirring constantly, for 2 to 3 minutes or until lightly browned. Stir in tomatoes, herbs de Provence, oregano, and crushed red pepper flakes, if desired. Bring tomato mixture to a boil; reduce heat to medium-low, and simmer for 30 minutes or until sauce thickens. Add salt and pepper to taste.

2. Prepare pasta according to package directions.

3. Bring tomato mixture to a boil, and add mussels, clams, and shrimp. Cook tomato mixture 5 to 6 minutes or until mussels and clams open and shrimp turns pink. Discard any clams and mussels that do not open.

4. Serve sauce over angel hair pasta with Italian bread.

NOTE: We tested with Pomi Strained Tomatoes and Pomi Chopped Tomatoes.

❝ I REMEMBER MY MAMA WAS ESPECIALLY GOOD AT MAKING SWEETS, LIKE BANANA PUDDING, AND BLACKBERRY AND PEACH COBBLERS, ❞ SAYS WILLIAM LEE GOLDEN.

ORANGE DREAMSICLE CAKE

makes: 12 servings   hands-on time: 50 min.
total time: 2 hours, 20 min, plus 24 hours to chill

★ ★ ★

William Lee Golden's sister, Lanette, passed down the recipe for this family favorite. His wife, Brenda, perfected it and now serves it often at dinner parties at their home, the Golden Era Plantation.

★ ★ ★

1	(10.25-oz.) box orange cake mix
1½	cups milk
½	cup vegetable oil
1	(3.4-oz.) box vanilla instant pudding mix
1	(3-oz.) box orange flavored gelatin
4	large eggs
1	(20-oz.) can crushed pineapple in syrup, drained
1	(8-oz.) container sour cream
8	oz. frozen grated coconut, thawed (about 2¼ cups)
1	(8-oz.) container frozen whipped topping, thawed

1. Preheat oven to 350°. Beat cake mix and next 5 ingredients at low speed of an electric mixer 30 seconds. Scrape down sides of bowl, and beat at medium speed 2½ minutes. Pour batter into 3 lightly greased and floured 9-inch round cake pans.

2. Bake at 350° for 20 to 25 minutes or until a wooden pick inserted in center comes out clean. Cool in pans on wire racks 10 minutes; remove from pans to wire racks, and cool completely (about 1 hour).

3. Pat drained pineapple with paper towels. Combine pineapple with sour cream and coconut; set aside 1 cup of mixture in a medium bowl. Spread remaining mixture between cake layers.

4. Fold whipped topping into reserved pineapple mixture. Spread over top and sides of cake. Cover cake, and chill 24 hours before serving.

NOTE: We tested with Duncan Hines Signature Orange Supreme Deliciously Moist Cake Mix.

MINISA SAYS, "THE KEY IS TO START WITH A COUNTRY CURED HAM THAT HAS BEEN AGED FOR A MINIMUM OF 12 MONTHS—THE OLDER THE BETTER."

MINISA'S COUNTRY HAM

makes: 36 servings (18 cups shredded ham)
hands-on time: 50 min.
total time: 8 hours, 20 min., plus 24 hours to soak ham

1   (12- to 14-lb.) uncooked   Butter
     country ham   Honey mustard
Biscuits

1. Place ham in a large container. Add water to cover, and soak 24 hours. Drain. Scrub ham 3 or 4 times in cold water with a stiff brush, and rinse well.

2. Place ham in a 7- to 10-gallon stockpot with water to cover, and bring to a boil over high heat. Reduce heat to medium-high, and simmer 3 to 4 hours, adding water as needed. Carefully drain. (Get someone to help you; the pot will be heavy!)

3. Preheat oven to 325°. Place ham, fat side up, in a large roasting pan. Cover with lid or aluminum foil.

4. Bake at 325° for 2 to 3 hours or until a meat thermometer registers 140°. Remove from oven to wire rack; cool completely (about 2 hours). Remove fat, and shred meat with 2 forks.* Chop meat, and serve on biscuits with preferred condiments.

*Cover and chill shredded ham in an airtight container 3 to 5 days or freeze 1 to 2 months.

★ ★ ★

All four members of The Oak Ridge Boys love this dish. Jim Halsey, who has been managing them for almost 40 years, and his wife, Minisa Crumbo Halsey, prepared it for a reception honoring the boys in Nashville.

★ ★ ★

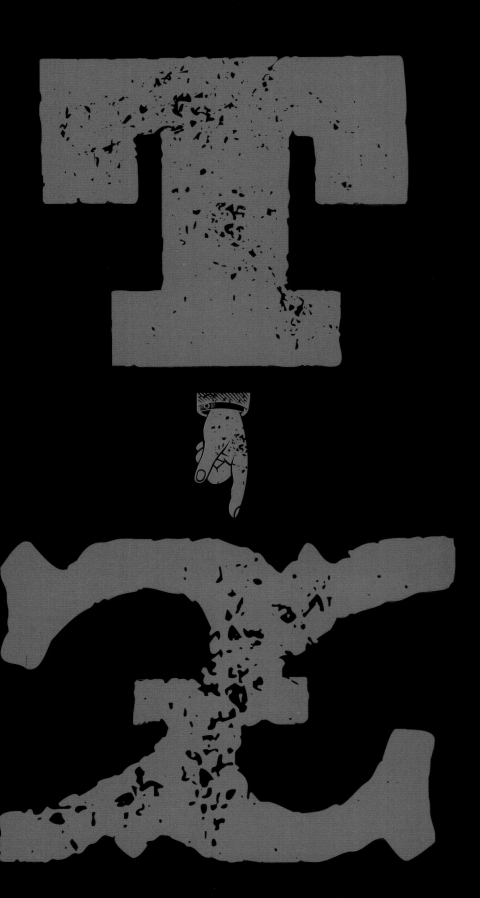

Randy Travis

Legendary country music artist Randy Travis has enjoyed an amazing, award-filled career that spans more than 25 years. His first gig in Nashville, however, was cooking in a kitchen.

When Randy Travis, who was born Randy Traywick, moved to Nashville in the early 1980s, he was rejected by every major record label. "They would say things like, 'It sounds okay. It's just that it's too country.' or 'That kind of music won't sell tickets or records,' " he told one interviewer.

At the time Randy had been singing for most of his life. He had grown up the second of six children on a farm in the small town of Marshville, North Carolina. While his father, Harold, wasn't a musician, the man enjoyed singing and instilled a love of music in Randy and his older brother, Ricky. He bought the boys guitars and paid for lessons so they could learn how to play them. Randy loved the music of Hank Williams and Gene Autry, and by the time he was 10, he and Ricky were playing at square dances, music competitions, and private parties. By 16, Randy was performing in clubs.

When he went to Nashville, he paid the rent by working as a short-order cook at the Nashville Palace, a dinner theater near the Grand Ole Opry. But it wasn't long before he began splitting his time between the Palace and the Opry, performing his "too country" music. In 1985, a record executive heard him play, recognized Randy's talent, and signed him. Not long after, he began performing under the name Randy Travis. "I am glad that I got turned down for as long as I did," he has said. "This is an interesting business, and

if I had been there as a teenager, signed and put on the road, I'm not sure I could have dealt with that much going on."

Randy's big break came in 1986 with the release of his first album, *Storms of Life,* which sold more than five million copies and featured the hits "On the Other Hand" and "Diggin' Up Bones." That same year, he was invited to become a member of the Grand Ole Opry. "Every time you walk on the Opry stage is a special feeling . . . it's just a wonderful energy on that stage," he has remarked.

Randy's storied career has now spanned more than a quarter of a century. He has sold millions of records, received numerous music awards (including seven Grammys), and earned a star on the Hollywood Walk of Fame. Through it all, Randy still professes an adage that is as true now as when he started singing. "The record business has changed a lot, but a good song is still a good song."

While he was getting his music career started in Nashville, Randy worked long hours at the stove, but he still loves to cook. Always in search of the perfect cuts of meat, he began raising buffalo on his Texas ranch, which he bought a couple of years ago. Randy has become known for making his signature Buffalo Tenderloin for friends and family—the meat is tender, flavorful, lean, and healthy. His go-to side dishes include Rosemary-Garlic Mashed Potatoes and Quick-and-Easy Hot-Water Cornbread.

~ albums & awards ~

Randy's debut album, *Storms of Life,* was released in 1986.

Randy Travis has sold more than 20 million records and has had 18 number-one singles and 29 Top 10 songs.

His awards include seven Grammys, 10 Academy of Country Music awards, 10 American Music Awards, and five Country Music Association honors.

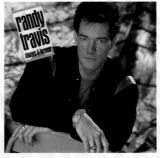

His second album, *Always & Forever,* includes the number one single "Forever and Ever, Amen."

RANDY HAS BECOME KNOWN FOR MAKING THIS SIGNATURE RECIPE FOR FRIENDS AND FAMILY—THE MEAT IS TENDER, FLAVORFUL, LEAN, AND HEALTHY.

BUFFALO TENDERLOIN

makes: 10 to 12 servings   hands-on time: 40 min.
total time: 1 hour, 30 min., plus 8 hours for chilling meat

This is a terrific dish to serve for a large dinner party, along with Quick-and-Easy Hot-Water Cornbread and Rosemary-Garlic Mashed Potatoes.

1	(5-lb.) buffalo tenderloin*	1½	Tbsp. freshly ground black pepper
¼	cup olive oil, divided	4	Tbsp. beef bouillon granules or 4 beef bouillon cubes
2	tsp. garlic powder		
1½	Tbsp. table salt		

1. Rub tenderloin with 2 Tbsp. olive oil, and sprinkle with garlic powder, salt, and pepper. Place in a large roasting pan; cover and chill at least 8 hours.

2. Preheat oven to 375°. Remove meat from refrigerator; let stand 30 minutes. Prepare bouillon according to package directions; set aside.

3. Cook tenderloin in remaining 2 Tbsp. hot oil over medium-high heat 15 minutes or until browned on all sides.

4. Bake at 375° for 30 to 35 minutes or to desired degree of doneness, pouring bouillon over tenderloin after 15 minutes. Remove from oven; cover loosely with aluminum foil, and let stand 15 minutes. Slice and serve with reserved pan drippings.

*Buffalo rib-eye loin or beef prime rib may be substituted for buffalo tenderloin.

TIP

If you can't get a large piece of buffalo tenderloin, you can halve the recipe or use beef instead.

IN THE EARLY DAYS OF RANDY'S CAREER, **HE PAID THE RENT WORKING AS A SHORT-ORDER COOK,** HONING HIS SKILL WITH SIDES LIKE THIS MOUTHWATERING RECIPE FOR MASHED POTATOES.

ROSEMARY-GARLIC MASHED POTATOES

**makes: 10 to 12 servings   hands-on time: 25 min.
total time: 1 hour, 35 min.**

4   medium-size garlic buds,
     cut in half crosswise
Heavy-duty aluminum foil
2   Tbsp. olive oil
4   sprigs fresh rosemary,
     cut in half
Table salt to taste

12   Yukon gold potatoes,
     unpeeled and cut into large
     cubes
1½   cups heavy cream
¾   cup unsalted butter
Freshly ground black pepper
     to taste

1. Preheat oven to 400°. Place bottom halves of garlic buds on 4 (12-inch) squares of heavy-duty aluminum foil, cut sides up, and drizzle with 1 Tbsp. olive oil. Top with rosemary sprigs, sprinkle with salt, and drizzle with remaining olive oil. Top with remaining garlic bud halves, cut sides down. Seal foil packets tightly. Bake at 400° for 40 to 45 minutes. Remove packets from oven; set aside to cool.

2. Bring potatoes, salt, and water to cover to a boil in a large Dutch oven over medium-high heat; cook 10 minutes or until potatoes are tender. Drain potatoes, and return to Dutch oven.

3. Squeeze roasted garlic cloves over potatoes; discard rosemary sprigs and garlic skins. Mash potatoes to desired consistency; set aside, and keep warm.

4. Heat cream and butter in a medium saucepan over low heat until butter melts. Stir cream mixture into potatoes. Add more salt and pepper to taste.

★ ★ ★

Enjoy this dish, as one of Randy's hit songs puts it, "forever and ever, amen!"

★ ★ ★

RANDY'S FRIENDS SAY THIS IS ONE OF THEIR FAVORITES, AND THEY GRAB EXTRA SLICES FOR THE TRIP HOME!

QUICK-AND-EASY HOT-WATER CORNBREAD

makes: 9 servings   hands-on time: 25 min.   total time: 35 min.

2   cups self-rising cornmeal mix

³⁄₄   cup extra light olive oil

1. Whisk together cornmeal mix and 2 cups boiling water in a medium bowl to make a thick batter.

2. Drop batter by one-quarter cupfuls into hot oil in a large heavy skillet over medium-high heat, and cook 1 to 1½ minutes on each side or until golden brown. Remove cornbread from skillet, and drain on paper towels. Add more oil as needed to fry remaining batter.

NOTE: We tested with Martha White's Self-Rising White Corn Meal Mix with Hot Rize.

★ ★ ★

This delicious cornbread only takes 5 to 8 minutes to make. It's great served au jus, with the pan juices from the Buffalo Tenderloin.

★ ★ ★

 **TIP**

This simple hot-water cornbread goes well with ham or fried fish, or served up with country-style scrambled eggs.

Hank Williams, Jr.

Born Randall Hank Williams, this singer-songwriter had little choice but to follow in his father's footsteps. Now an icon in his own right, Hank, Jr., has lived a life full of struggle and success.

"I had the greatest teachers in the world," Hank Williams, Jr., has said. Indeed, consider what it was like to take banjo lessons from bluegrass legend Earl Scruggs. Or to learn how to play the piano, boogie-woogie style, from a master. "Jerry Lee Lewis—I can see him at the piano, tellin' Mama, 'I'm gonna show this boy how it's done right,' " Hank Williams, Jr., once told an interviewer.

As the son of Hank Williams, Hank, Jr., seemed destined to follow in his daddy's path, one that presented just as many limitations as it did opportunities. "Other kids could play cowboys and Indians and imagine that they'd grow up to be cowboys," he wrote in his autobiography, *Living Proof*. "I couldn't do that. I knew I'd grow up to be a singer. That's all there ever was, the only option, from the beginning."

Hank Williams died when his son was just three years old. By eight, the boy began performing professionally, making his debut singing his dad's songs on a small stage in Swainsboro, Georgia. Three years later, Hank, Jr., took the stage at the Grand Ole Opry and sang his father's famous hit "Lovesick Blues." At 15, he had a six-figure-per-year recording contract, and his cover of his father's "Long Gone Lonesome Blues" was climbing the charts. But with Hank Williams's looming shadow, Hank, Jr., struggled to deal with the comparisons and criticism.

In the mid-1970s, the pressure proved too much, and he attempted suicide. In the wake of that near tragedy, he found his voice and sound. The new Hank Williams, Jr., style was pure country music overlaid with raucous Southern rock and blues. That sound led to his first million-selling album, *Whiskey Bent and Hell Bound,* released in 1979.

Throughout the 1980s and 1990s, Hank, Jr.'s, fame grew exponentially. With songs such as "Texas Women," "Dixie on My Mind," and "All My Rowdy Friends (Have Settled Down)," he won numerous awards, sold millions of albums, and became a household name. By the 2000s, he was recognized with lifetime awards that celebrated his stellar career, including CMT's Johnny Cash Visionary Award and his induction into the Nashville Songwriters Hall of Fame.

Along the way, he fostered a third generation of musicians. Two of his five children, Hank III and Holly, perform their own songs on stages around the world.

These days, Hank, Jr., still tours. When he's off the road, he splits his time between his homes in Paris, Tennessee, and Victor, Montana. He hunts wild game and has learned how to prepare it, making delicious elk beer chili and venison stews. As a side or even a meal itself, Hank, Jr., makes Cajun Rice Casserole, which includes bacon and okra. Classic with a slightly wild twist, Hank, Jr.'s, epicurean tastes are, as you would expect, right in stride with his style of music.

albums & awards

Hank, Jr., knows more than a little about "family tradition" as his 1979 album—a best-seller—with the same name attests.

Hank Williams, Jr., has had 10 number one singles, plus six platinum and 20 gold albums, with 13 of them reaching number one on the charts.

He's won numerous Emmy, Grammy, Academy of Country Music, CMT, and Country Music Association awards, including the CMT Johnny Cash Visionary Award in 2006.

Hank, Jr., was inducted into the Nashville Songwriters Hall of Fame in 2007.

Whiskey Bent and Hell Bound was also released in 1979 and became this country legend's first platinum album.

COUNTRY MUSIC'S GREATEST EATS

HANK, JR., HUNTS WILD GAME AND HAS LEARNED HOW TO PREPARE IT ALONG WITH DISHES LIKE THIS SPICY SIDE.

CAJUN RICE CASSEROLE

makes: 6 to 8 servings   hands-on time: 25 min.
total time: 1 hour, 25 min.

This tasty dish
has a Cajun kick,
reminiscent of Hank,
Jr.'s, Louisiana
birthplace.

½ lb. bacon, chopped
1   large onion, chopped
2   (16-oz.) cans diced tomatoes
    with juice
1   (10-oz.) can tomatoes and
    green chiles
½ lb. okra, trimmed and sliced
    ¼-inch thick
9   Tbsp. chopped fresh parsley
1   tsp. garlic salt
1   tsp. onion salt
Sea salt
Freshly ground black pepper
2   cups hot cooked long-grain
    rice

1. Cook bacon in a large skillet over medium heat, stirring often, 8 minutes or until crisp. Remove bacon, and drain on paper towels, reserving drippings in skillet. Add onion, and cook, stirring often, 5 minutes or until onion is tender and golden.

2. Add diced tomatoes and next 5 ingredients; bring to a boil. Reduce heat, and simmer over low heat, stirring occasionally, 45 minutes. Add salt and pepper to taste.

3. Serve over rice, and sprinkle with reserved bacon.

TIP

For even more flavor, use thick-sliced bacon.

Holly Williams

Holly Williams developed a love for cooking from her mother and grandparents. A member of the Williams country music royal family, Holly is making her own mark on the music scene with songs that are rich in story.

After touring and traveling thousands of miles, most artists might opt for lengthy one-on-one sessions with their favorite couch. Singer-songwriter Holly Williams prefers to step into her kitchen because cooking is the best way for her to unwind. "The first thing I want to do is invite people over and cook for them," she says.

It helps that she's got her dream kitchen. A few years ago, she and her husband, musician Chris Coleman, completely renovated the space to be open and functional. From nearly any spot in the room, she can easily reach what she needs. It's also configured so she can visit with guests or hang out with Chris while she is cooking. "I absolutely love cooking and eating and all things related to food," she continues. "I have such passion for spending hours at the stove with pans simmering."

That passion came from Holly's mother, Becky White Williams, and spending holidays with her maternal grandparents in the small community of Mer Rouge, Louisiana. "They were sweet country folk," she recalls. "They taught me the way of living simple." Her grandmother made delicious fried chicken, roast beef, and sides. And on the Fourth of July, they invited just about everyone in the community—sometimes as many as 250 people—over for barbecue, baked beans, and corn on the cob.

From her mother, Holly learned how to make simple, healthy dishes such as Tomato, Goat Cheese, and Arugula Frittata and Beach House Pasta, which was the perfect side to shrimp or fish while they vacationed down in the Florida Panhandle. Holly's aunt shared with her a recipe for Melting Moments,

albums & awards

Holly Williams' albums include *The Ones We Never Knew*, 2004, *Here with Me*, 2009, and *The Highway*, 2013.

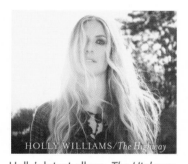

Holly's latest album, *The Highway*, was released in 2013, and includes "The Highway" and "Waiting on June."

one-bite sugar cookies topped with vanilla icing. "No other dessert on earth compares to them," she laughs. "We can't stop eating them all day."

Holly compares cooking to songwriting. "You choose your ingredients, you try and fail a few times and keep trying, you taste and test and taste and test, and the moment of finding the perfect mix for a recipe is equivalent to when I'm in the studio, and I hit on the perfect mix of words and music."

She was born into the music business. Her grandfather, Hank Williams, and father, Hank Williams, Jr., remain two of the most famous country musicians of all time. She embraced that legacy, but in her early 20s, she decided to create music on her own terms, edging away from her grandfather's classic country sound and her father's rowdy approach. Holly's songs are full of soothing melodies and well-spun stories, often about her family. "Waiting on June" recounts the heartbreaking, bittersweet life of her maternal grandmother, June Bacon White, and "Gone Away from Me," which is set in the Louisiana cemetery near her grandparents' hometown, pays homage to the lives of her forebearers.

To date, Holly has produced three albums, and she tours around the world nonstop. Her extensive travels present a hidden advantage. Inspired by the fashions she sees in the many places she visits, she opened a casual chic women's boutique called H. Audrey (her first initial and middle name) in Nashville, where she handles all the buying.

No matter whether she's happily busy with her boutique or in her kitchen, Holly says her music is and will always be her first love.

FINDING THE PERFECT MIX FOR A RECIPE IS EQUIVALENT TO WHEN I'M IN THE STUDIO AND I HIT THE PERFECT MIX OF WORDS AND MUSIC.

TOMATO, GOAT CHEESE, AND ARUGULA FRITTATA

makes: 6 servings   hands-on time: 35 min.
total time: 1 hour, 5 min.

6   large eggs
½   cup heavy cream
½   cup milk
Sea salt
Cracked black pepper
1   (4 oz.) package crumbled goat cheese

1   clove garlic, minced
¼   cup extra virgin olive oil
2   cups cherry tomatoes, halved
4   cups coarsely chopped arugula
Garnishes: arugula leaves, extra virgin olive oil

1. Preheat oven to 375°. Whisk together eggs, cream, and milk in a large bowl. Season as desired with sea salt and cracked pepper. Stir in goat cheese.

2. Cook garlic in hot oil in a 10-inch skillet over medium heat 1 minute or until lightly browned. Add tomatoes, and cook 3 minutes or until softened. Add arugula, and cook, stirring occasionally, 2 to 3 minutes or until wilted. Pour egg mixture over arugula mixture, and cook 5 minutes or until mixture begins to set.

3. Bake at 375° for 15 to 20 minutes or until the frittata is set and golden brown. Remove frittata from the oven, and let stand 5 minutes before serving.

★ ★ ★

This tasty dish is full of wonderful flavors and a variety of nutrients. You may think you are using much too much arugula, but be patient—it will cook down nicely.

★ ★ ★

" I ABSOLUTELY LOVE COOKING AND ALL THINGS RELATED TO FOOD. I HAVE SUCH PASSION FOR SPENDING HOURS AT THE STOVE WITH PANS SIMMERING. "

BEACH HOUSE PASTA

makes: 8 to 10 servings   hands-on time: 20 min.
total time: 4 hours, 20 min., including 4 hours for chilling

This easy pasta salad is the perfect dish to whip up when guests drop by unexpectedly.

1	cup finely chopped celery
1	cup finely chopped green bell pepper (optional)
1	(4.25-oz.) can chopped black olives
¼	cup chopped green onions
½	cup extra virgin olive oil
½	cup mayonnaise
1½	Tbsp. Creole seasoning
3	Tbsp. fresh lemon juice
1	(14.5-oz.) pkg. angel hair pasta, cooked

Garnish: celery leaves

1. Stir together celery, bell pepper, if desired, and next 6 ingredients in a large bowl. Add pasta; toss gently. Cover and chill for 4 hours.

TIP

Holly uses Tony Chachere's Original Creole Seasoning for just the right amount of spice for her family, but she suggests seasoning this dish to suit your palate.

HOLLY WILLIAMS

“THIS IS MY MOST FAVORITE DESSERT EVER, AND IT HOLDS SO MANY MEMORIES FOR ME OF FAMILY AND HOLIDAYS.”

MELTING MOMENTS

makes: 32 cookies   hands-on time: 40 min.
total time: 2 hours, 10 min., including Icing

1 cup butter, melted	1 Tbsp. sugar
2 cups all-purpose flour	Icing

1. Preheat oven to 300°. Combine butter, flour, and sugar in a bowl, and mix well. Shape dough into 1-inch balls. Place 2 inches apart on ungreased baking sheets. Press thumb in each cookie to make an indentation.

2. Bake at 300° for 20 to 30 minutes or until lightly browned. Cool 2 to 3 minutes on baking sheet. Press centers again with thumb while cookies are still warm. Remove to wire racks, and cool completely.

3. Spoon Icing into a zip-top plastic freezer bag; do not seal. Snip 1 corner of bag to make a small hole. Pipe Icing into center of each cookie.

ICING

makes: ¾ cup

1 cup powdered sugar	Pinch of table salt
2 Tbsp. melted butter	Additional milk
1 Tbsp. milk	Food coloring (optional)
1 tsp. vanilla	

1. Whisk together powdered sugar and next 4 ingredients in a small bowl, adding more milk as needed to reach desired consistency. Tint icing with 1 or 2 drops of food coloring, if desired.

★ ★ ★

These delicious thumbprint cookies are super simple to make. Have fun trying out different ways to decorate them.

★ ★ ★

TIP

When making a piping bag from a zip-top plastic bag, make sure to start by cutting a smaller hole than you think you'll need—you can always make it bigger.

Chris Young

At 20 years old, the singer caught the public's attention in 2006 by winning the competition reality show *Nashville Star*. Since then, he has scored a handful of number one singles and developed a love for a certain specially prepared steak.

When singer Chris Young was growing up, a visit to his maternal grandparents in Columbia, Tennessee, was guaranteed on every major holiday. "It was pretty much required," he says. "That's just the way Nanny and Granddaddy wanted it." They got what they wanted, but Chris got what he wanted as well—his grandmother's homemade cheese biscuits.

Everybody from the Young family—all the cousins, aunts, and uncles—cooked for these functions, and each brought one dish to share. The dish Chris always looked forward to was those biscuits. "They are simple, really," he says. "Just a regular biscuit—but with cheese and a whole bunch of butter."

These days, Chris is based in Nashville. The city has always been on his radar—he grew up in Murfreesboro, Tennessee, around 30 miles down the road—and music has been a major part of his life since he was small. He performed in children's theater productions and sang in high-school choirs. Just before he turned 21, Chris landed a spot on the music competition television series *Nashville Star*. That was 2006, and he won the competition that season, which earned him a record deal and launched his career. Since then, he has charted at least five number one singles, taken home a couple of American Country Music awards, and even scored a Grammy nomination.

albums & awards

Chris got his first break in 2006 when he won the 4th season of *Nashville Star*.

In 2010, Chris won the CMT Music Awards Nationwide Insurance Is On Your Side Award.

In 2011, he was named the American Country Awards Breakthrough Artist of the Year and won the Single of the Year Award for "Voices."

Chris released his fourth album, *A.M.*, in 2013.

That success translates into constant touring, so Chris doesn't get to do a whole lot of cooking. Every now and then, though, he'll start messing around in the kitchen. "I usually have to butcher something two or three times before figuring it out," he says with a laugh. And he's picked up some tricks from his mom, like marinating chicken in margarita mix and lime juice before grilling it.

However, if there's a special occasion—an event to celebrate, a date to impress—Chris sticks with his go-to restaurant, the Stoney River steakhouse on Nashville's west end. Chris eats there enough that he no longer needs a menu. The servers don't even ask: His dinner will definitely be the Coffee-Cured Filet Mignon with Stoney River Potatoes Au Gratin. Chris was initially turned off by the description of the steak, which is marinated in a mixture of coffee, molasses, and brown sugar. "It sounded terrible," he says. "Coffee? How was that going to work?" He said as much to a server, but she told him it was among their most requested entrées. Chris tried it and was hooked.

He also likes the restaurant's au gratin potatoes, which are made with shredded Gruyère cheese. "Of course they're going to be awesome," he says. "They're potatoes with cheese!" It's not too difficult to connect the dots here. "I think it goes back to that thing I've got with my grandma's cheese biscuits."

COFFEE-CURED FILET MIGNON

makes: 4 servings   hands-on time: 25 min.
total time: 2 hours, 40 min.

1½ cups boiling water	3 Tbsp. molasses
¼ cup instant coffee	3 Tbsp. olive oil
½ cup firmly packed dark brown sugar	2 tsp. ground cumin
⅓ cup kosher salt	4 (7-oz.) beef tenderloin filets
	Garnish: fresh rosemary leaves

1. Stir together boiling water and coffee in a medium bowl. Add sugar and salt, stirring until sugar dissolves. Stir in molasses and next 2 ingredients. Fill a large bowl half-full with crushed ice, and add 1 cup water. Place bowl of coffee mixture inside ice-filled bowl. Cool coffee mixture to room temperature, stirring occasionally.

2. Combine filets and marinade in a large zip-top plastic freezer bag, turning to coat. Seal and chill 2 hours, turning once. Remove steaks from marinade; discard marinade.

3. Preheat grill to 350° to 400° (medium-high). Grill, covered with grill lid, 5 to 7 minutes per side or to desired degree of doneness.

★ ★ ★

This incredible steak is Chris's favorite impress-a-date order when he's at the Stoney River restaurants in the Nashville area. Stoney River chefs Jim Filaroski and Michael Sabrin shared the recipe, adapted here for easy home cooking. Chris likes it with their potatoes au gratin and a glass of cabernet.

★ ★ ★

STONEY RIVER POTATOES AU GRATIN

makes: 4 to 6 servings (about 4 cups)   hands-on time: 35 min.
total time: 2 hours, 15 min.

2 tsp. melted butter	¼ tsp. ground nutmeg
2 tsp. minced garlic	4 oz. (1 cup) shredded Gruyère cheese
1 tsp. kosher salt, divided	1⅓ cups heavy whipping cream
1 tsp. freshly ground black pepper, divided	
2 lb. small baking potatoes, peeled	

1. Preheat oven to 350°. Brush butter on bottom of an 11- x 7-inch baking dish. Sprinkle garlic, one-third of salt, and one-third of pepper in bottom of dish.

2. Thinly slice potatoes lengthwise. Arrange one-half the potatoes in dish, slightly overlapping each slice. Season potatoes with one-half of remaining salt, one-half of remaining pepper, one-half of nutmeg, and one-half of shredded cheese. Repeat layers, placing potatoes in the opposite direction, ending with cheese. Slowly pour on cream.

3. Bake at 350° for 1 hour. Reduce oven temperature to 250°, rotate dish, cover with aluminum foil, and bake 30 minutes or until potatoes are tender and golden. Remove dish to a wire rack; let stand 10 minutes before serving.

Zac Brown Band

The Zac Brown Band stormed the country music scene in 2008 and has not rested on its laurels yet. The band founded Southern Ground, which supports numerous ventures outside music. "Generous" remains the best adjective to describe these guys.

Zac Brown likes giving," says Coy Bowles, the Zac Brown Band guitarist and keyboardist. "He likes making people feel good through food and music."

You see that generosity displayed during the "Eat and Greet" tour events the band hosts for fans before the show. Rusty Hamlin, executive chef for Southern Ground, the band's own record label, leads a team headquartered in its mobile kitchen nicknamed "Cookie." They set up a long buffet line, and Zac and the other band members literally serve the fans—often dishes like pork and beef tenderloins, coleslaw, biscuits with fig and agave butter and red-eye gravy, and braised Brussels sprouts—made fresh just for them.

The real treat is when Zac whips up a large batch of what he calls his "love sauce," which Coy says is like brown gravy with coconut that's a real crowd-pleaser. "They eat it, and the next thing you know, everybody is fat and happy and 'hanging out' together," Coy explains. "It's a way for us to be one-on-one with the fans. We hear their stories and stay connected."

Coy adds that these events also keep the band humble. Rusty agrees. "Pictures and autographs are a little empty," he notes. "A plate of food across the table has so much more substance."

On the day of an Eat and Greet, Rusty tries to buy as much locally grown produce and other foods available in the town where they're playing. "It's amazing when you can feed people something that fresh, that's been out of the ground less than 24 hours." As he's building his menus, Rusty—who also works with two restaurants in the Atlanta area—relies on his roots. He grew up in Baton Rouge, Louisiana, and from a young age watched his mother cooking in

The band's big break came in 2008 with the song "Chicken Fried," which reached number one on the country music charts.

the kitchen. When he was in high school, he worked in the seafood department in a local grocery store, slinging crawfish and more. After culinary school, he worked as a line cook in Louisiana. That's why Louisiana Blue Crab-Stuffed Catfish Fillets with Bacon-Mushroom Stone-Ground Grits and Cajun Rémoulade is one of his favorite dishes to prepare. "My style of food is anywhere from the west side of Louisiana (the seafood) all the way to Georgia (the bacon) and the Carolinas (the grits)," he says.

Zac is a pretty good cook, too, adds Rusty. He particularly likes a dish Zac makes by smoking pork rib meat and then finishing it on the grill. "It's Pork 2.0," he says.

These days, with Rusty in tow and the Eat and Greets, the band rarely, if ever, misses a good meal. "When you have access to that food, it's amazing," says Coy. "I have to watch eating too much of it, though, because nobody likes to see a fat guy rock out."

What you may not know is that before Zac Brown was The Zac Brown—recognized universally by his trademark bushy beard and knit hat—he owned a restaurant for a while near Lake Oconee, east of Atlanta. At Zac's Place, he cooked and served many of his own recipes. It was an early venture for the young musician who grew up in North Georgia and began performing at clubs throughout the state in the early 2000s. "I know how to get my hands dirty, and I think knowing what that means absolutely can help you as a songwriter," Zac has said, "because if you never know anything else but music, then you expect to be taken care of. I've been the person I write about in my music since day one."

Back then, he was formulating his sound, which is often compared to James Taylor, Dave Matthews,

(continued on page 242)

"HE DOESN'T REALLY HAVE TO HAVE THE ZAC BROWN BAND. I THINK HE WOULD BE SUCCESSFUL JUST AS ZAC BROWN. BUT THE BAND ADDS A LOT AND TAKES IT TO ANOTHER LEVEL. IT'S ONE BIG FAMILY WITH HIM."

THE BAND EATS WELL ON THE ROAD THANKS TO CHEF RUSTY HAMLIN, WHO MANS A MOBILE KITCHEN AND HELPS THE BAND HOST "EAT AND GREET" EVENTS.

and Jimmy Buffet. After the 2008 hit "Chicken Fried" shot to number one on the country charts and went quadruple platinum (selling more than 4 million copies), the band rose with meteoric speed and has continued a steady musical evolution, making fun-fueled, Southern rock and country infused with bluegrass and occasional outliers, such as reggae and Caribbean. The band has grown to seven members, some of them from Georgia, playing multiple instruments. Zac also founded an umbrella company called Southern Ground that is comprised of everything from a music label and festival to

a metal shop, custom leather shop, and a film and video production company.

But as the machine that is the Zac Brown Band brand continues to churn, reports recounting Zac's big-hearted personality surface over and over again. "One cool thing about Zac is that he loves to include everybody," emphasizes violinist and singer Jimmy De Martini. "He doesn't really have to have the Zac Brown Band. I think he would be successful just as Zac Brown. But the band adds a lot and takes it to another level. It's one big family with him."

The Zac Brown Band has plenty of love to go around—lucky fans are invited to join this rolling minstrel show (above), where the food is good and the company is better.

Even the menu for "Southern Ground Grub" is rendered by hand (top right) and features artisanal Southern classics with a twist.

⮜ albums & awards ⮞

2009: Grammy Award for Best New Artist, CMT Music Awards *USA Today* Breakthrough Video of the Year for "Chicken Fried," and the Academy of Country Music Award for Top New Vocal Duo or Group

2010: Country Music Association Award for New Artist of the Year

2011: CMT Music Award for Performance of the Year for "Margaritaville" with Jimmy Buffett, Grammy Award for Best Country Collaboration with Vocals for "As She's Walking Away" (featuring Alan Jackson), Academy of Country Music Award for Top Vocal Event of the Year for "As She's Walking Away" (featuring Alan Jackson)

2013: Grammy Award for Best Country Album for *Uncaged*

The Zac Brown Band's 2008 album *The Foundation* includes the number one hit song "Chicken Fried."

Uncaged, released in 2012, features singles with Trombone Shorty and Amos Lee.

> **MY STYLE OF FOOD IS ANYWHERE FROM THE WEST SIDE OF LOUISIANA (THE SEAFOOD) ALL THE WAY TO GEORGIA (THE BACON) AND THE CAROLINAS (THE GRITS),** SAYS CHEF RUSTY.

LOUISIANA BLUE CRAB-STUFFED CATFISH FILLETS

makes: 6 servings   hands-on time: 1 hour, 5 min.
total time: 2 hours, 15 min., including Bacon-Mushroom Stone-Ground Grits and Cajun Rémoulade

8	Tbsp. butter
1	small onion, diced
1	small green bell pepper, diced
3	celery ribs, diced
1	Tbsp. minced garlic
1	Tbsp. fresh lemon juice
2	tsp. Cajun seasoning, plus more to taste
1/8	tsp. hot sauce, plus more to taste
1/2	lb. fresh lump blue crabmeat, drained

1 cup panko (Japanese breadcrumbs)
6 (7-oz.) fresh catfish fillets
1 tbsp. olive oil
Table salt to taste
Freshly ground black pepper to taste
Bacon-Mushroom Stone-Ground Grits
Cajun Rémoulade

1. Melt butter in a large skillet over medium-high heat; add onion and next 3 ingredients, and cook, stirring often, 5 minutes or until onion is translucent. Add the lemon juice, 2 tsp. Cajun seasoning, and 1/8 tsp. hot sauce, and cook 1 minute. Add crabmeat, breadcrumbs, and additional Cajun seasoning and hot sauce, if desired. Remove from heat; cool to room temperature.

2. Preheat oven to 400°. Butterfly catfish fillets by making a lengthwise cut in 1 side, cutting to but not through the opposite side; unfold.

3. Spoon stuffing crab mixture evenly down center of 1 side of each butterflied fillet; fold opposite side over stuffing.

4. Brush fillets with olive oil; sprinkle with salt and pepper. Place fillets on a lightly greased baking sheet. Bake at 400° for 15 to 20 minutes or until done. Serve with Bacon-Mushroom Stone-Ground Grits and Cajun Rémoulade.

★ ★ ★

Chef Rusty Hamlin feeds the Zac Brown Band members and their fans at big "Eat and Greet" suppers when the band is on tour. Here's one of Chef Rusty's favorite dishes, served with Bacon-Mushroom Stone-Ground Grits and Cajun Rémoulade.

★ ★ ★

BACON-MUSHROOM STONE-GROUND GRITS

makes: 6 servings   **hands-on time: 25 min.**
total time: 1 hour, 15 min.

8 oz. smoked bacon slices, chopped	½ cup heavy cream
3 Tbsp. minced garlic	2 Tbsp. butter
2 cups chicken broth	Table salt to taste
2 cups milk	Freshly ground black pepper to taste
1 cup uncooked white stone-ground grits	1½ cups (6 oz.) shredded white Cheddar cheese
8 oz. wild mushrooms, chopped	6 green onions, chopped

1. Cook bacon in a medium saucepan over medium heat, stirring occasionally, 7 to 8 minutes or until crisp. Remove bacon, and drain on paper towels, reserving 2 Tbsp. drippings in skillet.

2. Cook garlic in hot drippings over medium-low heat, stirring constantly, 1 minute. Transfer garlic and drippings to a small bowl; set aside. Wipe saucepan clean with paper towels.

3. Bring chicken broth and milk to a boil in saucepan over medium heat. Slowly whisk in grits. Reduce heat to low, and simmer, stirring often, 25 to 30 minutes or until grits are softened and smooth.

4. Add mushrooms, cream, butter, and salt, and pepper to taste. Cook, covered, over medium-low heat, stirring occasionally, 10 minutes or until mushrooms are softened. Remove from heat; add cheese, green onions, and reserved bacon, garlic, and drippings. Serve immediately.

CAJUN RÉMOULADE

makes: 2 cups   **hands-on time: 20 min.**   **total time: 20 min.**

½ cup dill pickle relish	2 Tbsp. minced garlic
½ cup mayonnaise	2 Tbsp. Creole mustard
¼ cup diced onion	2 Tbsp. prepared horseradish
¼ cup diced celery	3 dashes hot sauce
¼ cup diced red bell pepper	2 Tbsp. fresh lemon juice
¼ cup chopped fresh parsley	Table salt to taste
3 Tbsp. ketchup	Freshly ground black pepper to taste
3 Tbsp. yellow mustard	

1. Pulse all ingredients in bowl of a food processor 30 to 40 seconds or until finely chopped. Cover and chill any leftover sauce up to 3 days.

metric chart

The recipes that appear in this cookbook use the standard U.S. method for measuring liquid and dry or solid ingredients (teaspoons, tablespoons, and cups). The information in the following charts is provided to help cooks outside the United States successfully use these recipes. All equivalents are approximate.

METRIC EQUIVALENTS FOR DIFFERENT TYPES OF INGREDIENTS

A standard cup measure of a dry or solid ingredient will vary in weight depending on the type of ingredient. A standard cup of liquid is the same volume for any type of liquid. Use the following chart when converting standard cup measures to grams (weight) or milliliters (volume).

Standard Cup	Fine Powder (ex. flour)	Grain (ex. rice)	Granular (ex. sugar)	Liquid Solids (ex. butter)	Liquid (ex. milk)
1	140 g	150 g	190 g	200 g	240 ml
³/₄	105 g	113 g	143 g	150 g	180 ml
²/₃	93 g	100 g	125 g	133 g	160 ml
¹/₂	70 g	75 g	95 g	100 g	120 ml
¹/₃	47 g	50 g	63 g	67 g	80 ml
¹/₄	35 g	38 g	48 g	50 g	60 ml
¹/₈	18 g	19 g	24 g	25 g	30 ml

USEFUL EQUIVALENTS FOR LIQUID INGREDIENTS BY VOLUME

¹/₄ tsp			=	1 ml	
¹/₂ tsp			=	2 ml	
1 tsp			=	5 ml	
3 tsp	=	1 Tbsp	=	¹/₂ fl oz	15 ml
		2 Tbsp	=	¹/₈ cup	=	1 fl oz	30 ml
		4 Tbsp	=	¹/₄ cup	=	2 fl oz	60 ml
		5¹/₃ Tbsp	=	¹/₃ cup	=	3 fl oz	80 ml
		8 Tbsp	=	¹/₂ cup	=	4 fl oz	120 ml
		10²/₃ Tbsp	=	²/₃ cup	=	5 fl oz	160 ml
		12 Tbsp	=	³/₄ cup	=	6 fl oz	180 ml
		16 Tbsp	=	1 cup	=	8 fl oz	240 ml
		1 pt	=	2 cups	=	16 fl oz	480 ml
		1 qt	=	4 cups	=	32 fl oz	960 ml
				33 fl oz	=	1000 ml	=1 l

USEFUL EQUIVALENTS FOR DRY INGREDIENTS BY WEIGHT

(To convert ounces to grams, multiply the number of ounces by 30.)

1 oz	=	¹/₁₆ lb	=	30 g
4 oz	=	¹/₄ lb	=	120 g
8 oz	=	¹/₂ lb	=	240 g
12 oz	=	³/₄ lb	=	360 g
16 oz	=	1 lb	=	480 g

USEFUL EQUIVALENTS FOR LENGTH

(To convert inches to centimeters, multiply the number of inches by 2.5.)

1 in				=	2.5 cm		
6 in	=	¹/₂ ft		=	15 cm		
12 in	=	1 ft		=	30 cm		
36 in	=	3 ft	=	1 yd	=	90 cm	
40 in				=	100 cm	=	1 m

USEFUL EQUIVALENTS FOR COOKING/OVEN TEMPERATURES

	Fahrenheit	Celsius	Gas Mark
Freeze water	32° F	0° C	
Room temperature	68° F	20° C	
Boil water	212° F	100° C	
Bake	325° F	160° C	3
	350° F	180° C	4
	375° F	190° C	5
	400° F	200° C	6
	425° F	220° C	7
	450° F	230° C	8
Broil			Grill

Index

ARTISTS

ISBN-13: 978-0-8487-4297-3
ISBN-10: 0-8487-4297-4
Library of Congress Control Number: 2014933413

Printed in the United States of America
First Printing 2014

Oxmoor House
Vice President, Brand Publishing: Laura Sappington
Editorial Director: Leah McLaughlin
Creative Director: Felicity Keane
Art Director: Christopher Rhoads
Senior Brand Manager: Daniel Fagan
Senior Editor: Erica Sanders-Foege
Managing Editor: Elizabeth Tyler Austin
Assistant Managing Editor: Jeanne de Lathouder

Southern Living Country Music's Greatest Eats
Project Editor: Emily Chappell Connolly
Senior Designer: Melissa Clark
Executive Food Director: Grace Parisi
Assistant Test Kitchen Manager: Alyson Moreland Haynes
Recipe Developers and Testers: Wendy Ball, R.D.; Tamara Goldis, R.D.;
    Stefanie Maloney; Callie Nash; Karen Rankin; Leah Van Deren
Food Stylists: Victoria E. Cox, Margaret Monroe Dickey,
    Catherine Crowell Steele
Photography Director: Jim Bathie
Senior Photographer: Hélene Dujardin
Senior Photo Stylist: Kay E. Clarke
Photo Stylist: Mindi Shapiro Levine
Assistant Photo Stylist: Mary Louise Menendez
Senior Production Managers: Greg A. Amason, Sue Chodakiewicz

Southern Living
Editor: M. Lindsay Bierman
Creative Director: Robert Perino
Managing Editor: Candace Higginbotham
Executive Editors: Hunter Lewis, Jessica S. Thuston
Deputy Food Director: Whitney Wright
Senior Food Editor: Julie Grimes
Test Kitchen Director: Robby Melvin
Test Kitchen Specialist/Food Styling: Vanessa McNeil Rocchio
Test Kitchen Professional: Pam Lolley
Recipe Editor: JoAnn Weatherly
Assistant Editor: Hannah Hayes
Style Director: Heather Chadduck Hillegas
Director of Photography: Jeanne Dozier Clayton
Photographers: Robbie Caponetto, Laurey W. Glenn, Hector Sanchez
Assistant Photo Editor: Kate Phillips Robertson
Photo Coordinator: Chris Ellenbogen
Senior Photo Stylist: Buffy Hargett Miller
Assistant Photo Stylist: Caroline M. Cunningham
Photo Administrative Assistant: Courtney Authement
Editorial Assistant: Pat York

Time Home Entertainment Inc.
President and Publisher: Jim Childs
Vice President, Brand and Digital Strategy: Steven Sandonato
Vice President, Finance: Vandana Patel
Executive Director, Marketing Services: Carol Pittard
Executive Director, Retail and Special Sales: Tom Mifsud
Executive Publishing Director: Joy Bomba
Publishing Director: Megan Pearlman
Director, Bookazine Development and Marketing: Laura Adam
Associate General Counsel: Helen Wan

Contributors
Author: Tanner Latham
Editor: Nichole Aksamit
Recipe Developer and Tester: Susan Gilpin
Copy Editor: Norma Buttersworth-McKittrick
Proofreaders: Lauren Brooks, Barry Smith
Indexer: Mary Ann Laurens
Photographer: Ashley Hylbert
Photo Assistant: Beth Roth
Food Stylist: Mary Carter
Photo Stylist: Priya Mani
Hair and Makeup Artist: Nichole Lim
Fellows: Ali Carruba, Sarah Duffy, Elizabeth Laseter, Amy Pinney,
    Frances Higginbotham, Madison Taylor Pozzo, Deanna Sakal,
    April Smitherman, Megan Thompson, Tonya West

Acknowledgments & Special Thanks

I am grateful to the many people who worked long hours to create this project. Specifically, I would like to thank Daniel Fagan for the opportunity, Erica Sanders-Foege and Nichole Aksamit for their collective guidance and patience, Susan Gilpin and the other test kitchen professionals who measured every ingredient, and Norma Buttersworth-McKittrick for her meticulous attention to detail.

To the country stars and personalities, thank you for your openness. Your stories are the foundation of this book. To their publicists, thank you for your tireless persistence.

I thank my unbelievably wonderful family, because they are the only people I know who are more excited about this book than I am. I feel that support every day.

And I extend a very special thanks to Jennifer Davick, the love of my life, for inspiring me at every step and enduring all the early mornings. We're making it happen.

—Tanner Latham

We'd also like to thank...

From CMT, Alicia Bequette, Donna Duncan, Cindy Finke, Jacklyn Krimmel Jones, Peter Mannes, Anne Oakley, and Amanda Phillips, as well as Kay West, who was instrumental in bringing all of these great artists on board for this book.

Photo Credits

Robbie Caponetto: 108, 226, 248-9

CMT: 28, 48, 75, 270-1

Daniel Fagan: 262, 263 (Center), 264-5, 266

Getty Images: 18, 29, 160, 164, 238, 255

Kristy Belcher Photography: 83

Laurey W. Glenn: 176

David Hanson: 2

Michael Hanson: 7, 8, 9, 272

Russ Harrington: 152, 180

Ashley Hylbert: 11 (Bottom Center), 34, 35, 36, 37, 38-9, 40, 82, 84-5, 87, 144, 145, 146-7, 190-1, 192-3, 194-5, 196

Brian Lazzaro: 98

Krista Lee: 28

David McClister: 222

Art Meripol: 11 (Lower Left)

Monarch Publicity/Bigger Picture Entertainment: 42

Amber Richards: 267

Chris M. Rogers: 259

Hector Sanchez: 6 (Top Center), 68, 92, 256-7

Jeff Sciortino: 198

Randee St. Nicholas: 234

Southern Reel: 239, 240-1, 242-3

Beth Studenberg: 74

Angela Talley: 170

Adam Taylor: 116

Suzanne Teresa: 24

Charles Walton: 11 (Bottom Right)

Warner Music Nashville: 5, 122

Webster and Associates Public Relations and Marketing: 214

Jim Wright: 60, 134

Kate York: 140

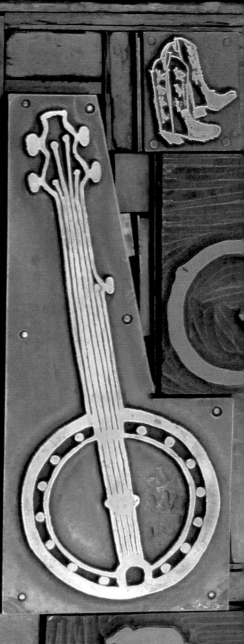

About Our Cover, a Hatch Show-Print Original

Take a look at the cover of this book and you'll see that it's a showstopper in its own right. Crafted by the respected Hatch Show Print shop, our cover—and the poster that announces the arrival of this wonderful project—was put together by the best in the business.

When we began discussing the cover design for our book, we knew we wanted it to capture the spirit of country music and Nashville. So, there was no doubt in our minds that we had to hire the renowned Hatch Show Print shop, a letterpress print shop that has been a fixture in Music City for 135 years.

Hatch produces about 600 printing jobs per year for stars like Shania Twain, Ricky Skaggs, and The Mavericks. They have also created designs for everyone from Bob Dylan to Bruce Springsteen to B.B. King. Unbeknownst to many, the shop also designs labels for companies like Nike, Taylor Guitars, and Jack Daniel's, as well as album covers, show posters, and book covers like ours. As we quickly discovered, their process hasn't changed much since the days when they were just starting out. And that's just how the designers and printers who work there like it. "Hatch is a dream job," says Amber Richards, who took on our project.

"We take our design skills and then create something beautiful by hand," she continues. "We keep this process and the history of the place alive." When we approached Hatch with

Designer-printer Amber Richards and shop manager Celene Aubry of Hatch Show Print in Nashville, Tennessee

★★★★★

our cover copy and a few design ideas, Amber rendered some sketches. She then dove into the archive—135 years worth of letters and hand-carved images. She selected 20 different wooden block type faces, all in the Western style, then winnowed them down to the one that, according to her, had the perfect antique look and classic feel for our book.

Once Amber had the design form set, she took it to a press, locked it in, and cranked the print through three times, once for the color red, once for the color yellow, and once for turquoise accents. "We like to say the designer is the printer, and the printer is the designer," Amber remarks. "We follow the job all the way through and have complete ownership of it. People are always surprised that the whole process is done by hand from start to finish."

The design was then scanned and digitized, so that it could be scaled and submitted for printing with the rest of the book. When it was all finished, Amber broke apart the blocks for our cover and poster designs and filed each piece back into the archive, knowing full well that it might be another 135 years before they are used again.

"WE FOLLOW THE JOB ALL THE WAY THROUGH AND HAVE COMPLETE OWNERSHIP OF IT. PEOPLE ARE ALWAYS SURPRISED THAT THE WHOLE PROCESS IS DONE BY HAND FROM START TO FINISH."

After 135 years in five different locations around downtown Nashville, Hatch Show Print moved to 224 5th Avenue South, which features a large, custom-designed print shop. We watched the poster for our book roll right off the presses at the previous lower Broadway location (above). Once it was blocked (opposite page, top left), the colors were added one at a time, after the type was inked (opposite page, top right and bottom left) for the dynamic result.

 **VISIT**

Hatch Show Print
224 5th Avenue South, Nashville, TN
615-256-2805
hatchshowprint.com

ABOUT OUR COVER

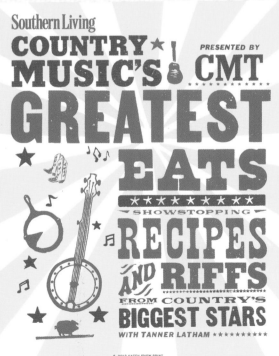

COUNTRY MUSIC'S GREATEST EATS

About CMT

When it comes to country music and entertainment, CMT is the fans' number-one source. A unit of Viacom, CMT (and cmt.com) reach more than 92 million homes in the U.S. Top talent and an unparalleled mix of music, news, live concerts, and series are available on the 24-hour music channel, CMT Pure Country, CMT Mobile, and CMT VOD.

About the author

Tanner Latham was born into a family of storytellers and grew up in a small town in Northeast Alabama nestled in the foothills of the Appalachian Mountains. Stories, of course, were sacred—best shared at supper tables or on screened porches.

As travel editor for *Southern Living*, he wrote about distinctly Southern destinations, from cinder block barbecue joints to luxurious, five-star resorts. He has also worked as a reporter for NPR in Charlotte, North Carolina, producing on-air stories, slideshows, and multimedia videos. He is currently the content director for Trevelino Keller, a public relations firm in Atlanta, Georgia. In his spare time, he hosts "Authentic South," (AuthenticSouth. com) a storytelling podcast that explores Southern culture through food, art, travel, music, and the fascinating characters who define the region.